# The Nursery

## *in a weekend*

# The Nursery

*in a weekend*

# Roo Ryde

**BETTERWAY BOOKS**

CINCINNATI, OHIO

To Daniel. Thank you darling for being so patient during the months of preparation in getting this book together; the weekends that the house was taken over for photography and the nights I sat up writing. My hero. My love.

# Acknowledgments

A big thank you to Dominic Blackmore for his great photography and laid-back approach; A.D., the hottest salsa dancer around; Gayle Scott of Blinkers Designs, the only person I know who can translate my design talk into reality. And my heartfelt thanks also to Sara Colledge at Merehurst for having the faith to come back to me a second time! Howard Romain for his magic touch with a paintbrush and also to Gill Thomas. And finally, my beautiful mum, Marian, who makes the best assistant that any daughter could ask for—I can't thank her and dad enough for their help and support.

Please note that all small objects used in these projects should be kept out of the reach of babies and small children and that you should be sure that all materials used conform to health and safety regulations.

Distributed to the trade and craft markets in North America in 2002 by
Betterway Books
an imprint of F&W Publications, Inc.
4700 East Galbraith Road
Cincinnati, OH 45236
(800) 289-0963

ISBN 1-55870-619-4

Editor: Geraldine Christy
Designer: Anthony Cohen
Photographer: Dominic Blackmore
Stylist: Roo Ryde
Artwork: King & King
Commissioning Editor: Sara Colledge
Publisher: Anne Wilson

Color separation by Bright Arts, Hong Kong
Printed in Singapore by Tien Wah Press

# Contents

# Introduction

Whatever age you are I bet that when you hold a baby in your arms your heart melts. Even if you do not have a baby yourself, you are sure to know someone who does. Welcoming a newborn into this world with a whole selection of new goodies is what every proud parent would like to do, but unfortunately practicality kicks in. Few of us have the ways or means to give our new baby a completely brand-new start to life—that is, a fully fitted-out nursery complete with new accessories.

There are certain items, however, that are invaluable in a nursery to help make your life a little bit more organized and easier—such as a baby changing unit that can house all the bottles and lotions that you need at hand when changing a diaper; a diaper stacker to hold all the diapers, and a big roomy laundry bag for all those dirty little outfits—three or four changes a day can be common! And what about a comfortable rocking chair that you can relax in when feeding the baby? It is not just about making the nursery look good, but about getting it organized and making things easier for yourself.

So thank goodness for friends, family, and secondhand stores, all of which can offer an assortment of furniture that has usually seen better days. But do not worry, because this is where the fun begins. This is the time to use your imagination. You do not have to be particularly creative. If you have never picked up a paintbrush in your life, do not be afraid. It is never too late to start.

"Face lifting" a room and "making over" furniture are definitely buzz words these days. Time and resources are such precious commodities that we all want to learn the shortcuts, the quick and easy route. With that in mind, the projects in this book are designed to be entirely practical, easy to follow, and to culminate in fabulous results.

A few words of caution—do not rush into a project! I cannot over-emphasize the importance of preparation. That involves not just making sure that you have everything that you will need to complete a project, but also doing any necessary prep work to whatever item or surface you may be working on. If you remember to do this before you start, you should have no problems. Also, do not be put off by the stunning look of any project and think that you could never achieve it; you really need no formal training to complete any of the projects in this book.

Each project has been broken down into a number of steps, but if you know a better or faster way of achieving something, feel free to follow your instincts. Use the projects as inspiration, but also follow your personal taste. If you want to use other colors or fabrics, do so. If they need to fit into an existing scheme, alter them accordingly. Each project is extensively illustrated with easy-to-follow step-by-step instructions and you will also find further tips and practical suggestions. You may find that some of the projects will take up most of your time over a weekend, while others can be completed more quickly.

All the materials that I use—especially paints and varnishes—are nontoxic. I cannot stress enough the importance of checking that all products you use are suitable for babies, especially when painting a cradle or crib. Likewise, make sure that anything that is anywhere within reach of your baby has no loose parts on it that could be pulled off and swallowed.

Turn each project into an enjoyable experience—I can guarantee you that after all the effort you put in you will stand back at the end of the day and be very proud of your new creations.

Good luck and have fun.

# Laundry bag and diaper stacker

*This attractive laundry bag and diaper stacker provide a place to put dirty washing and handy storage for a pile of clean diapers just where you need them.*

### Planning your time

**DAY ONE**
**AM:** Cut out the pieces for the diaper stacker and hem the edges

**PM:** Machine sew the pieces together and add the eyelets

**DAY TWO**
**AM:** Cut out all the pieces for the laundry bag and hem the edges

**PM:** Machine sew the pieces together and add the eyelets

### Tools and materials

Each item needs 1⅔yds (1.5m) of fabric (look for wipe-clean plasticized fabrics—these are often used to make tablecloths and are readily available from fabric stores)

**Metal eyelet kit**

**Hammer**

**Piece of scrap wood for hammering on**

B abies wear diapers until the age of two or three during the day and probably longer, until they are confidently dry, at night. So you will need to keep a constant supply close at hand and in something that you can conveniently reach into with one hand if necessary.

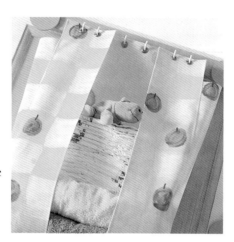

And over the first couple of years of a baby's life—you may have to cope with a few outfit changes every day, and that mounts up to a lot of dirty laundry. You will need a large roomy bag to put it all in.

Both the diaper stacker and laundry bag have been made using the same principle. The diaper stacker merely differs in its front opening, which allows easy access to the diapers. Both were made out of plastic-coated cotton, which has the added benefit of being washable. This type of fabric is a little more difficult to work with than regular cotton fabric, so make a practice run on your sewing machine first. It is advisable to use a heavy-duty needle and, where possible, machine sew from the wrong (uncoated) side of the fabric.

Eyelets provide an easy hanging system. They are relatively simple to use and can be bought in kits from fabric stores. Do not be tempted to insert them while working on your tabletop, however, because they will mark it. Use a scrap of wood as a surface and work on the floor.

# Day One

## Step 1

For the diaper stacker (shown here in yellow checked fabric) cut out:
One piece of fabric 12x24" (30x60cm) for the back piece (A)
Two pieces of fabric 6x21" (15x52cm) for the side pieces (B)
Two pieces of fabric 6x24" (15x60cm) for the front pieces (C)
One piece of fabric 6x12" (15x30cm) for the bottom piece (D).

## Step 2

Start working on the diaper stacker. Hen the top edges of all the main body pieces: A, B, and C. Then hem the two edges that will become the front opening edges on pieces C.

## Step 3

Machine sew all the widths together using a straight stitch on the wrong side of the fabric. Start with piece A and sew pieces B to either side of A. Then sew pieces C to either side of pieces B.

## Step 4

With the right side of the fabric facing you, top stitch each of the four seams using a straight stitch.

## Step 5

Pin the base piece D to the bottom of the main body, right sides together, and then place the bottom of the bag onto the sewing machine and sew it on. Clip to angle each corner so that when you turn the bag right side out each corner will be neat and sharp.

### Using plastic-backed fabric

Plastic-backed fabric is now readily available. It is more often than not fronted by a cotton fabric.

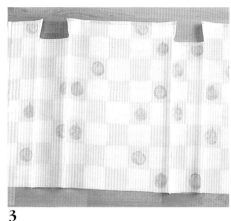

1

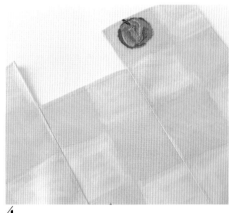

2

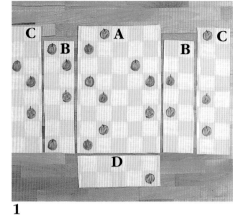

3

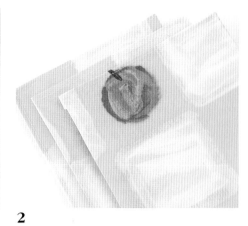

4

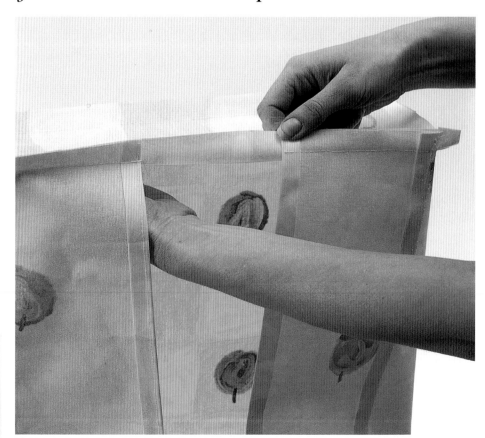

5

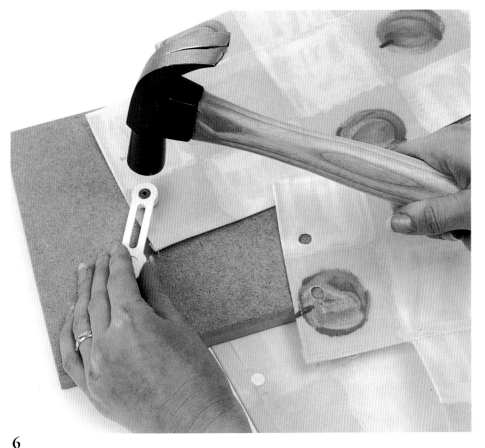

6

7

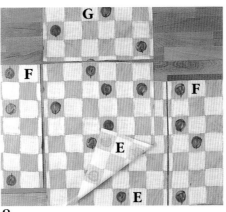

8

9

## Hanging up the bags

To hang the laundry bag and diaper stacker I used simple cup hooks. These I inserted into a wooden board, which I painted in a bright color and attached to the back of a door.

## Step 6

Using a pencil, mark six equally spaced dots along the top edge of the bag approximately ¾" (2cm) in from the edge. Remember to do this on both sides of the bag. The holes must line up exactly when the front and back are in line with each other. The diaper stacker has a front opening, so you will end up with four eyelets along the front pieces and six along the top of the back piece. Place the fabric over a piece of wood, then place the eyelet hole maker on a pencil mark and firmly hammer it to cut out the hole. Continue this until all the holes have been cut.

## Step 7

Each eyelet consists of two metal pieces. Place the hole over the deeper metal ring and then set the other metal ring on top of it, so that the material is sandwiched in between. Then place the eyelet tool over the rings and hammer firmly. This secures the two pieces of the eyelet together.

## Day Two

## Step 8

For the laundry bag (shown here in green checked fabric) cut out:
Two pieces of fabric 18x28" (45x70cm) for the back and front pieces (E)
Two pieces of fabric 10x25" (25x62cm) for the side pieces (F)
One piece of fabric 10x18" (25x45cm) for the bottom piece (G).

## Step 9

The green checked laundry bag has been taken through the same stages as the diaper stacker except for the fact that the front is one piece. Once its top edges have been hemmed and the front and back (E) have been sewn to the sides (F), creating a tube, the base piece (G) is sewn on as in Step 5. Then insert the eyelets (Steps 6 and 7 above).

# Fun window treatment

*Window dressing is an art in itself and this fun treatment will transform the look of the nursery. Small windows can be made to look bigger and large windows will look more welcoming.*

For a baby's room, tab-top curtains are an excellent choice—they will not use a lot of fabric and they can easily be backed with blackout lining if you wish. You also do not need to use any curtain tape. The tabs of the heading are treated as a design feature, and so are the curtain rod and, obviously, the fabric. All need to be considered as part of the overall design when you are selecting them.

Chunky wooden curtain poles with simple end finials are perfect to complete the look. Opt for plain wood ones that can be painted to fit in with your color scheme.

The curtains I designed feature a valance at the top, which is a great way of introducing a contrast fabric, but if you want to simplify the project you can leave it out.

The addition of the cheesecloth blind softens the window and it has been given a design twist by turning it into an Austrian blind. Gently gathering up the fabric highlights its pom-pom fringe.

Measuring is a crucial part of curtain making. It is worth spending time getting this right because if you end up with curtains that are too short or too narrow you will notice your mistake every time you walk into the room.

If you are working with a patterned fabric remember to try to match the pattern across the pair of curtains. To achieve this effect, each width of fabric must be cut so that the pattern elements are in the same place.

## Planning your time

**DAY ONE**
**AM:** Cut out the curtains, lining, and tabs; machine sew together the tabs

**PM:** Machine sew the curtains and linings, then hand sew them together

**DAY TWO**
**AM:** Machine sew on the contrast flap and attach the tabs

**PM:** Cut and make the cheesecloth blind

## Tools and materials

Fabric for the main curtains and tabs

Lining for the curtains

Contrast valance fabric

Curtain weights

Needle and thread

Pom-pom fringe for the valance

Cheesecloth

Mini pom-pom fringe for the cheesecloth

Eight metal rings

Three metal screw eyes

Length of 1" (2.5cm) wooden board the width of the window

Length of Velcro the width of the window

5½yds (5m) of curtain string

Acorn (pull-cord stopper) and cleat

Scissors

Slim wooden board for bottom of the cheesecloth panel (optional)

**1**

## Day One

### Step 1

Cut out all the pieces of fabric. For the main curtains, measure the finished drop that you want and then add 10" (25cm) hem allowance. Bear in mind that the final drop of the curtain must include the 4" (10cm) drop of the tabs. The measurements for the linings will be exactly the same as for the main curtains. The contrast valance needs to be one-fifth of the curtain drop (including seam allowance) and the material for each tab measures 4½x9" (11x22cm), giving you a 4" (10cm) tab. Make a minimum of nine tabs per curtain. Also, bear in mind any pattern repeats when you are measuring, which may mean you will have to use extra fabric.

### Step 2

Sew together all the fabric widths. This will include the curtain fabric widths, the lining fabric widths, and the valance widths.

### Step 3

Make all the tabs. To make a tab, fold the fabric in half lengthwise, right sides together, and sew ½" (1cm) from the edge. Turn it right side out and press the tab with a warm iron, making sure the seam runs down the center of the tab.

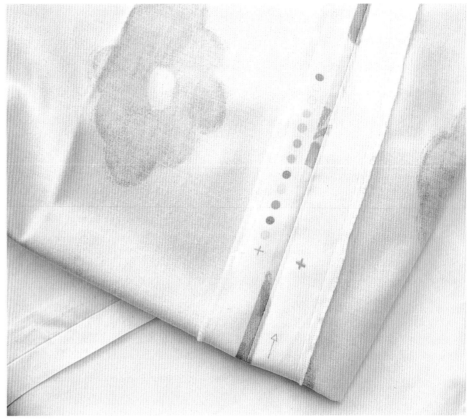

**2**

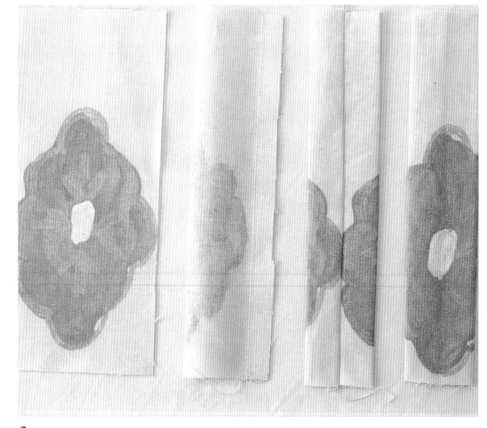

**3**

4

5

6

## Step 4

Take the lining fabric and turn over a ½" (1cm) hem and press with an iron, then turn over 3¼" (8cm) more and machine stitch all the way along the hem and press. Fold over ¾" (2cm) down each side and press.

## Step 5

On the curtain fabric turn over 4" (10cm) all the way along the bottom and press with an iron and then turn over 4¾" (12cm) more and press. Hand sew the hem with a slip or hem stitch. Turning over these amounts will help to give the curtains weight at the bottom. Press in 2¾" (7cm) down each side. You do not need to hem the sides since they will be hidden by the linings. If you are using curtain weights, now is the time to attach them in each corner before sewing up the corners.

## Step 6

Place the lining on the curtains wrong sides together and hand sew down the sides and along the bottom. Leave the top open.

### *Using up leftover fabric*

There is usually fabric left over from pattern matching and it is ideal for making tab tops, tiebacks, or matching cushions for the room.

7

## Day Two

### Step 7

Take the valance fabric and turn in ½" (1cm) along the bottom edge and press with an iron. Pin the pom-pom fringe to the back of the fabric along the turn-up, then machine stitch it on.

### Step 8

Take the finished tabs and pin them equally spaced along the top of the curtain on the lining side, facing downward. Make sure that the seam side of each tab is facing the lining. Machine stitch along each tab so that it is securely held in place on the curtain.

### Step 9

Take the valance with its hemmed bottom with trim attached and place it so that its right side is facing the sewn-on tabs and lining. Machine stitch a straight line all the way along the top edge, joining the curtain and valance together. When completed, simply flip over the valance; the tabs will pop up and the curtain is finished!

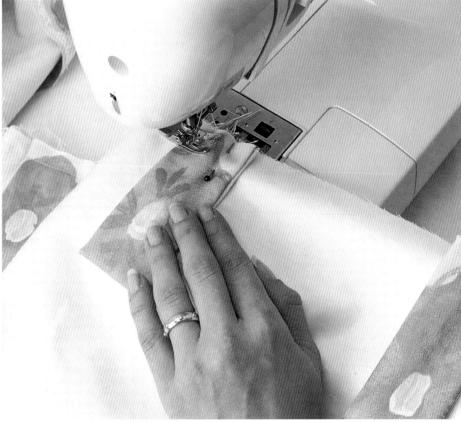

8

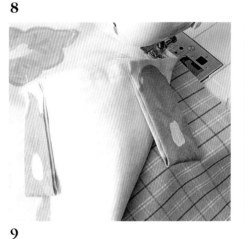

9

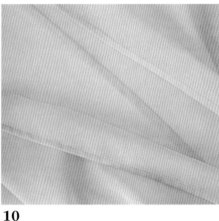

10

### Step 10

Measure the width of your window and add 2½" (6cm) for seam allowances on the width and drop of the cheesecloth. Cut the cheesecloth into three pieces, with the center piece being double the width of the two side pieces. Machine sew the widths together with French seams and hem the side edges.

### *Hanging the curtains*

When threading the tabs onto the wooden pole leave one tab at the outside edge to go on the far side of the bracket supporting the rod. It will hold the curtain in place and keep the outer edge from being pulled into the middle of the pole.

**11**

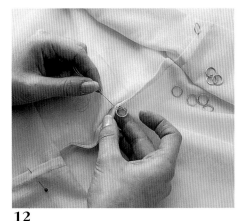

**12**

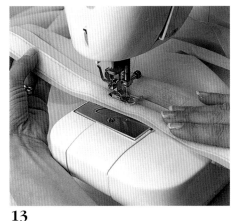

**13**

## Step 11

Turn over ½" (1cm) all the way along the bottom edge of the cheesecloth and press with a warm iron, then turn over 1½" (3.5cm) more and machine stitch this to form a channel on the wrong side. Pin the pom-pom fringe onto the bottom edge of the right side and machine stitch it in place. The reason for creating a channel is to give two finished dressing options to the blind—with and without a wooden board.

## Step 12

Along the two middle seams, hand sew four metal rings at equal intervals onto each seam.

## Step 13

Fold and press ¾" (2cm) all the way along the wrong-side top edge of the cheesecloth. Take one side of the Velcro strip and machine stitch it onto the pressed edge. Machine sew two lines along the top and bottom edge of the Velcro.

## Step 14

Staple the other side of the Velcro to the wooden board and lay the board and cheesecloth panel out on the floor. Where the two middle seams meet the board, screw in a metal eye. Also screw in an eye 1½" (4cm) from one of the ends—this will dictate which side the pulley will be on. Then take a piece

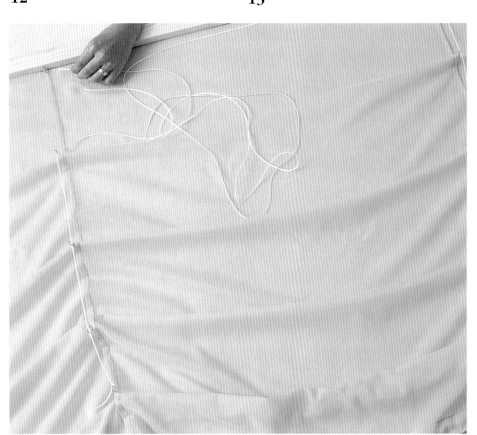

**14**

of string and knot it securely to the bottom ring and thread it up through the rings, up into the eye on the board, and along through the second and third eye on the baton. Then similarly take another piece of string up through the other row of rings up to the (second) eye on the board and along to the third, end eye. Now you should have two strings to the ends of which you must attach the acorn (pull-cord

stopper). Get someone to help you hold the baton up to the window. Unfasten the Velcro on the cheesecloth, but hold the cheesecloth up as it is attached via the strings. Screw the baton into the window frame, then refasten the blind with the Velcro.

Attach the cleat to the side where the strings will hang and pull the blind into the desired position.

# Painted glass mobile

*This mobile will fascinate even the youngest of babies with its variety of bright colors and shapes. Suspended from the ceiling, it provides a kaleidoscope of changing patterns.*

One of the first things a baby does is to focus on strong colors and mobiles are an excellent way of attracting a baby's attention. Your baby will spend many hours fascinated by the slow movement of its parts. Most store-bought mobiles tend to clip onto the side of the crib, but I wanted to create one that could be hung from the ceiling.

Using glass for the components is not as difficult as it may sound. Most hardware stores are more than happy to cut out glass shapes—as long as the pieces are relatively simple. Do make sure the finished mobile is safely out of the baby's reach; do not suspend it directly above the crib. If you would prefer not to use glass in the nursery, you could use Perspex shapes instead.

Glass outliner paints come in tubes and take a little practice to work with; you hardly need to squeeze the tube when applying it. Keep your hand steady by resting it on a flat surface. If you do make a mistake, simply wipe it off with a piece of tissue. The outliner paint needs to be left overnight to harden up and once hard it is difficult to remove.

Glass paints are easy to work with and a little goes a long way. They are available in a wide array of colors and you certainly will have no problems if you are trying to color match something.

Once you have attempted some glass painting and realized how easy it is to achieve fantastic results, you'll want to paint all the plain glass surfaces in your home!

## Planning your time

**DAY ONE**

**AM:** Cut out the templates and get glass shapes cut

**PM:** Paint the gold outlines

**DAY TWO**

**AM:** Paint glass pieces with the colors and allow to dry

**PM:** Thread beads and glass pieces together and construct the mobile

## Tools and materials

A sheet of styrofoam (available from art suppliers)

Craft knife and cutting mat

Glass shapes cut by a hardware store

Glass outliner and colored glass paints

Lacquer thinner

Small paintbrush

Assortment of glass or plastic beads and jewelry wire

1yd (1m) of braided cord in five colors

Scissors

1

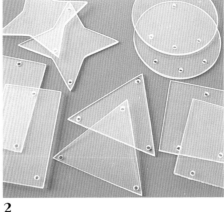

3

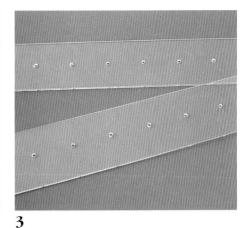

2

## Day One

### Step 1

Decide on the shapes that you want for your mobile. I used very simple ones—a square, circle, triangle, star, and rectangle. Templates for these are on page 76. Enlarge them on a photocopier. Draw them onto sheet styrofoam and cut them out using a craft knife. Mark on them with a pen where any holes need to be drilled.

### Step 2

Take the styrofoam shapes to your local hardware store and get the store assistant to cut out five of each shape. (You could use fewer, it just depends how long you want each "droplet" to be.) After the store assistant has drilled all the holes into them, make sure that he or she smooths off all the edges. This leaves the shapes with all blunt sides so that they are safe.

4

### Step 3

You will also need to have two pieces of glass cut that measure 2½x12" (6x30cm) with seven evenly spaced holes running down the middle of them. These will form the base through which the whole mobile is threaded together.

### Step 4

Using the glass outliner, gently draw a design onto each glass shape. I echoed the shape of each design but there is no reason why you cannot draw something completely different. Allow the shapes to dry overnight and let the outlines harden. The purpose of using the outliner paint is that when it is dry it prevents the glass paints from running into each other, thus enabling the use of different colors.

### *Choosing glass paints*

There are a variety of glass paints available from craft shops, but to ensure that the light will shine through your mobile make sure that you select paints that have a transparent finish.

# Day Two

## Step 5

Lay all the pieces out on a covered work surface, and working with one paint color at a time, randomly paint the shapes and strips. To change color rinse the brush out with lacquer thinner. When finished, allow the pieces to dry for a couple of hours.

## Step 6

Pick out the shapes that will hang at the bottom of each droplet and thread on an assortment of beads using jewelry thread. Knot them securely in place. Continue until all the lowest shapes have beads attached.

## Step 7

Using jewelry wire, attach each droplet of five shapes together. Thread the wire through a few times to ensure that all the pieces are securely held.

## Step 8

Lay the two strips of glass one on top of the other so that the middle hole on each one is centered. Poke a long piece of thread through the middle hole and bring it up over a corner and then down through the center hole again. Then bring the thread up over a different corner and down through the center hole again. Repeat this until the two pieces are firmly attached together. You will end up with a cross shape.

## Step 9

Using colored braid, tie a double knot into one end, and thread this into the top hole on a droplet, then thread it into an outside hole on the cross. Weave the braid in and out of the holes along the cross until it comes up near the center hole. Thread up all the droplets, then tie a secure double knot with all five braids. Secure the knot with a few stitches, attach a hook to the ceiling, and suspend your mobile!

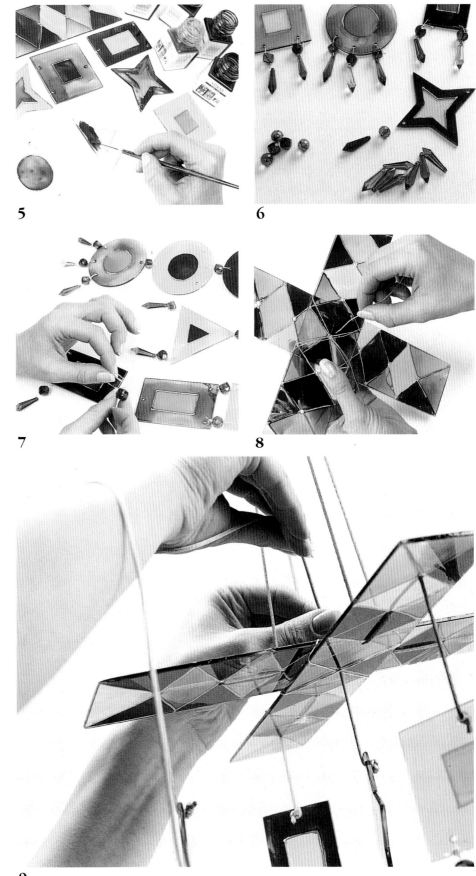

5

6

7

8

9

# Baby changing unit

*This useful unit has lots of drawers to keep all the bits and pieces you need when changing the baby and enough space for the baby to lie on.*

A piece of furniture that is custom made to your requirements can be a costly investment, so thank goodness for the increased popularity of particle board. You can buy it in a variety of thicknesses at almost any home improvement store. It is made out of wood pulp that is then compressed together to form sheets and is very easy to work with. It creates a great deal of dust when cut, however, so wear a mask.

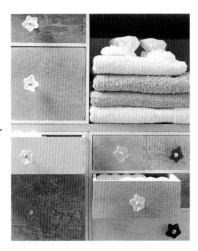

If you do not feel confident enough to cut the pieces yourself, simply take the dimensions of all the pieces that are needed for this project to a home improvement store where they will cut it for you.

When formulating the size of your changing unit remember that the top surface must be large enough for a baby to lie on with room either side for the bottles and toiletries that you will need when changing diapers.

I made the depth of the shelves large enough to house some self-contained, unfinished wooden storage boxes. These can be bought so inexpensively that it is not worth spending the time or money trying to make drawers for the unit.

The outer frame was painted in a solid color since particle board has no grain. However, the little drawer fronts were decorated with a spray color wash. These paint sprays are very easy to use and the finished effect reveals the grain and brings out the beauty of the wood.

The finishing touch is provided by the attractive colored-glass handles. These make all the difference, so it is worth spending a little time searching for unusual accessories.

## Planning your time

**DAY ONE**
**AM: Cut out the particle board pieces and build the changing unit**

**PM: Prime the whole unit**

**DAY TWO**
**AM: Paint the unit in your chosen colors and spray the drawer fronts**

**PM: Varnish the unit and drawers; allow to dry; drill holes and screw in the handles**

## Tools and materials

¾" (18mm) thick particle board

Jigsaw and dust mask

Power drill

Pencil, ruler, and tape measure

Sanding block

Hammer and small tacks

All-purpose spackle

Six 2½" (65mm) butt hinges (plus screws)

One can of quick-drying primer and undercoat paint

Paintbrushes

Two shades of latex paint—1 quart can of the main color and a ½ pint can of the secondary color

Selection of storage boxes or drawers

Spray cans of acrylic color wash

Handles for the drawer fronts

Acrylic varnishing wax

Wood glue

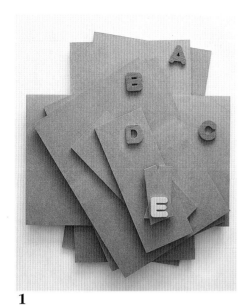

**1**

## Day One

### Step 1

Cut out the particle board pieces for the frame of the unit. You will need:

Two pieces 20x34¾" (50x88cm) for the side supports (A)

Two pieces 20x27½" (50x70cm) for the shelves (B)

One piece 20½x33" (52x84cm) for the top piece (C)

Two pieces 20½x8" (52x20cm) for the side flaps (D)

Two wedge-shaped pieces with flattened ends for the flap supports (E). The straight edge of the pieces should measure 8" (20cm), the wide end 4" (10cm), the narrow end 2" (5cm), and the sloping edge 8¼" (21cm).

### Step 2

Mark with a pencil all the pieces that need cutting. Using a jigsaw and wearing a dust mask, support the pieces of particle board on a surface and cut them to size.

### Step 3

Sand down all the edges of the pieces to smooth them all off. Wear the dust mask and work in a well-ventilated area.

**2**

**3**

## Step 4

Take the side pieces (A) and measure 11½" (29cm) in from both the top and bottom and draw two lines that are ¾" (20mm) apart. These mark where the shelves will sit. Repeat this on both side panels and mark a point in the center and then two points about 1½" (4cm) in from both edges. Also take the top piece (C) and lay a shelf on it, center it, and mark the sides—this will give you the positions for the side panels.

## Step 5

Drill holes on the pencil-marked points, making sure that you countersink the holes. You will need three holes along each pencil line. Thus, you will have six holes on each side panel and six on the top piece. Also, drill three pilot holes into the top edge of the side uprights (A); this will help when you screw the top onto the sides.

## Step 6

In order to aid assembly, lightly hammer in some tacks along the pencil line in pairs opposite each other. These will help to position and hold the pieces together while screwing. These must be removed after assembly!

## Step 7

Take a side panel (A) and sit it on top of the ends of both shelves. Use the tacks to hold them in place. Apply a line of wood glue along the edge, screw in the screws along the sides, and then remove the tacks. Repeat this with the other side panel. Then stand it upright and apply a line of wood glue on each side panel edge. Place the top piece on top and screw it in the edge of the side uprights.

## Step 8

Spread a little all-purpose spackle over the screw heads to disguise them. Remove any excess and allow to dry.

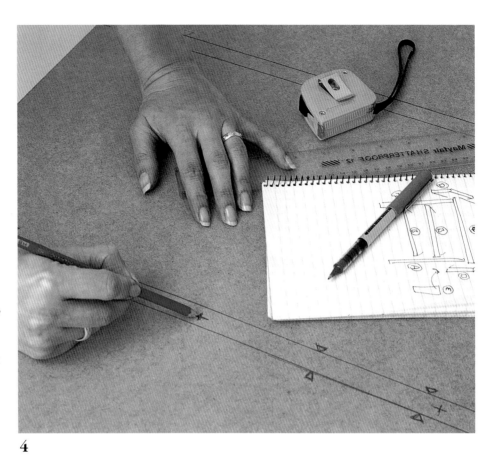

4

5

6

7

8

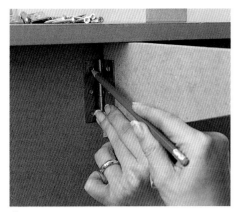

9

## Step 9

Take the flap support (E), and using
a 2½" (65mm) butt hinge, mark off
where the screws are to go. Pilot drill
the holes first; then, screw the hinge
in place. The flap support should be
12¾" (32cm) from the front edge
and 7" (18cm) from the back edge and
butting up to the top piece.

## Step 10

Take the flap (D) and mark where the
two hinges are to go—2¾" (7cm) in
from the edge on each side. Pencil
mark around a hinge and cut out a slot
for it on the flap side. This means when
you close the hinges they will sit flush.
Repeat this for the hinge on the other
side. Screw into place.

## Step 11

The photograph shows the unit with
the drawers slotted into place. For the
finished unit I turned the drawers
back to front.

10

11

## *Using different drawers*

The distance between the shelves has
been calculated to accommodate a
particular type of storage box. It is not
vital to use the boxes, however, and you
may prefer to design alternative shelving
solutions without drawers.

**12**

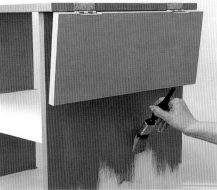

**13**

**14**

**15**

**16**

## Step 12

Give the whole unit a coat of quick-drying primer and undercoat paint. Remember to paint the undersides of shelves and flaps. Allow to dry.

## Day Two

## Step 13

Decide on your color scheme and paint the whole unit with latex paint and then allow to dry. I also used latex to paint the sides of the drawers. Gently sand the unit down to produce a really smooth finish.

## Step 14

Using a combination of different colors of spray color wash, gently spray the backs of each drawer. The reason I used the backs is that they do not have finger ridges cut into them. But you could use this type of drawer the right way around and save the bother of attaching handles.

## Step 15

Mark a center point on each drawer front and drill a hole for the handle.

## Step 16

Using acrylic varnishing wax, apply a coat to the whole unit and the drawer fronts. When this is dry (approximately two hours) it can be buffed for a gentle sheen. Finally, screw on the handles.

## *Gluing for strength*

Wood glue is used to give the unit extra strength and stop any movement that might occur.

# Cow crib bumper and comforter

*This cow crib adds fun to bedtime and daytime naps as well as acting as a friendly companion without the need for lots of soft toys.*

There is no reason why crib accessories cannot be given the "magic touch." Traditional satin and lace crib quilts and bumpers are usually very plain, though contemporary ones in bright colors are available. But I had never seen anything really exciting, so I created this lovable cow, who I am sure you will soon grow to love.

I used washable cotton fabrics that are also slightly textured, which makes them more durable than plain sheeting. The exception to this is the underside of the comforter, which can be made in plain sheeting.

I have included templates for all the small face pieces on pages 70 and 71—you should find that they will work with any size crib. It is very important when making the bumper to be sure that all the parts are extremely well sewn together so that constant tugging will not work them loose. When making the comforter you might find it easier to leave out the shaped bottom end and simply square it off. Either way it should still look the part!

Once you have mastered this project you could go on to make other adorable creatures. How about a pink piggy, a white cat, or an orange tiger!

## Planning your time

**DAY ONE**

**AM:** Cut out the bumper pieces; construct the hooves, horns, and ears

**PM:** Make the nose and hand sew onto the face; make the piping and attach to both sides of the bumper; machine sew two sides of the bumper together

**DAY TWO**

**AM:** Cut out the comforter pieces; appliqué on the patches

**PM:** Attach the tassel; sew the two sides together; sew the hoof detail and turn right side out

## Tools and materials

White cotton fabric

Black cotton fabric

Pink corduroy fabric

Brown corduroy fabric

4oz (115g) cotton batting

One small black tassel

## Day One

### Step 1

Cut out the pieces for the crib bumper.

For the main piece, measure the width of your crib and add 12" (30cm) each side. The highest point in the center measures 14" (35cm) and the narrower ends measure 8" (20cm). Cut two of these main body pieces, and cut another piece the same shape out of 4oz (115g) batting.

Cut four hooves out of black fabric, each measuring 5½x8" (14x20cm).

Cut five ties, each measuring 2x32" (5x80cm), out of black fabric.

Cut four patches out of black fabric.

Using the templates on pages 70 and 71:

Cut four horns out of brown fabric.

Cut four ears—two out of pink fabric and two out of black fabric.

Cut two eye bases out of white fabric.

Cut two black pupils out of black fabric.

Cut one main head piece out of black fabric.

Cut one head segment piece out of white fabric.

Cut one top of nose and one bottom of nose out of white fabric.

1

### Step 2

Appliqué the hooves and patches onto both the front and back crib bumper pieces. Lay the batting behind the white piece of fabric that will become the front piece and attach this when appliquéing on the black parts. The hooves are placed at each end, while the patches can be randomly placed. Simply machine sew around them using a zigzag stitch.

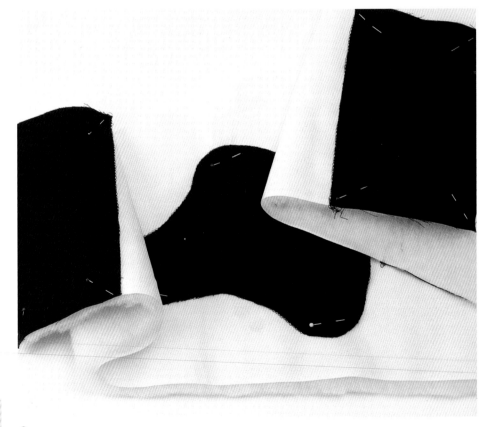

2

### *Safety*

It is very important that a crib bumper is not used with a baby under one year old. Also, it is vital that all the pieces are securely machine stitched in place.

**3**

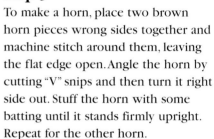

**5**

## Step 3

To make a horn, place two brown horn pieces wrong sides together and machine stitch around them, leaving the flat edge open. Angle the horn by cutting "V" snips and then turn it right side out. Stuff the horn with some batting until it stands firmly upright. Repeat for the other horn.

## Step 4

To make an ear, take a pink and black ear piece and place them wrong sides together. Machine sew around them, leaving the flat edge open. Angle them by cutting little "V" snips and then turn the ear right side out. Pinch the bottom edge together and machine stitch it to hold it in this pinched position. Repeat.

## Step 5

Construct the face by appliquéing the pupils of the eyes onto the whites of the eyes. Then take the black main head piece and smaller white head segment, turn under the sides of the white piece, press with an iron, and appliqué it onto the center of the black piece. Then appliqué the whites of the eyes onto either side of the face. Finally, place the face onto the top center of the front bumper and pin the ears and horns in place, putting their open ends under the face. Appliqué all the way around the face, making sure that you attach the ears and horns.

**4**

## Step 6

Machine sew the darts on the top nose section. Then, at the inner point of each dart, hand sew a few stitches with black thread to create a nostril. Place the right sides of the nose pieces together, sew around the outer curve, angle the seam by cutting little "V" snips, and turn it right side out. Then stuff the nose with some of the batting.

## Step 7

With the batting firmly packed inside the nose, pin the nose in position directly under the eyes on the face. Sew it in place all the way around, then remove the pins.

## Step 8

Make up the ties from black fabric. Take a strip and fold in both the sides to the center, then fold this strip in half and sew it all the way down the edge to form a neat tie. Repeat for all ties.

## Step 9

Machine stitch the ties on. Fold them in half lengthwise and pin four along the front piece of the bumper and one on the back piece. Machine stitch them firmly in position.

## Step 10

Place the right sides of the bumper together and machine stitch all the way around, leaving about 10" (25cm) along the bottom edge through which to turn it. To create the full effect of the hooves, simply machine stitch up the middle of each hoof and down again to form a very slim "V" upside down. Then cut into this "V."

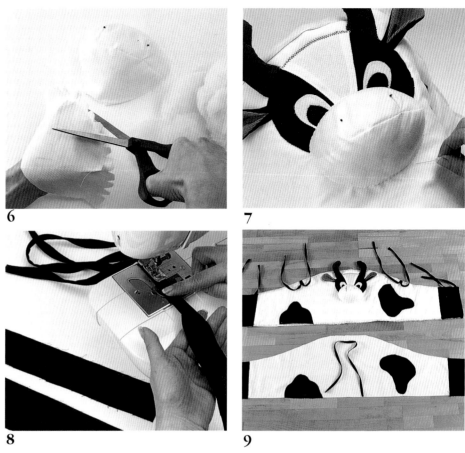

6

7

8

9

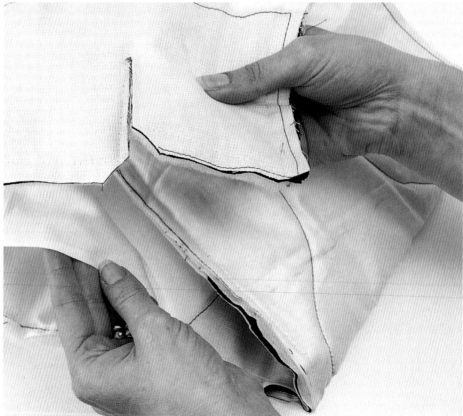

10

11

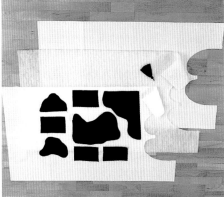

12

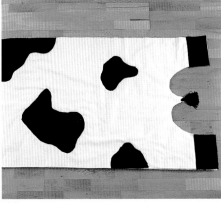

13

## Step 11

Turn the bumper right side out and hand sew the opening.

## Day Two

## Step 12

Cut out all the pieces for the crib comforter.

Measure the crib width and add 4" (10cm), and measure the crib length and subtract 4" (10cm). This measurement will be the size of the overall comforter. Cut out two of these pieces in white fabric and then cut the "M" shape into one end. Cut exactly the same shape out of the batting.

Cut four hooves out of black fabric, each measuring 4¾x7" (12x18cm).

Cut four patches out of black fabric.

You will also need one small black tassel for the tail.

## Step 13

Place the top comforter piece on top of the batting and machine sew on the hooves and appliqué on the patches. Also machine stitch the tassel in place at the point on the "M" shape.

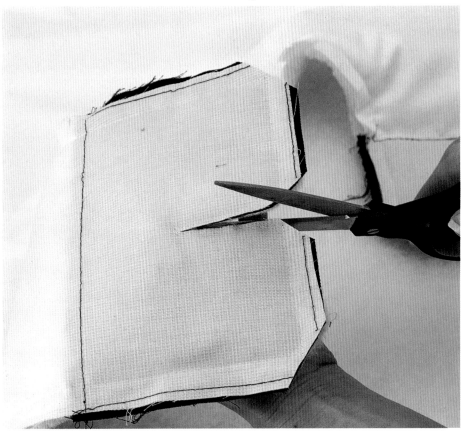

14

## Step 14

Create a sandwich with the top of the comforter (padding already attached) and the plain underside of the comforter. Place them right sides together and machine sew all the way around, leaving about 10" (25cm) along a straight edge through which to turn it. Turn the comforter the right side out and hand sew the opening. Machine the slim "V" into each hoof and cut.

### Easy ways of working

An easy way of appliquéing, as used here, is to use a zigzag stitch and catch in all the raw edges of the fabric.

When using the batting to stuff the ears, horns, and nose you may find it easier to shred it first in between your fingers.

# Palm tree height chart

*Measure your baby's growth against this height chart. Older brothers and sisters will enjoy helping you and seeing how much bigger they have grown too!*

When babies are tiny and newborn it is hard to imagine them ever growing up. Yet only six weeks later they are smiling at you; by nine months they are sitting up; and around their first birthday they are taking a few faltering steps. So while they are shooting up, what better way of keeping a record than a height chart?

The trunk of the palm tree is made from a piece of particle board that was softly shaped down its edges with a penknife. Be careful when doing this, as it necessitates a slow nicking action to create a slightly rippled edge.

The palm leaves, monkeys, and bananas are made out of felt. Felt is an easy fabric to work with and requires no hemming around its edges. Felt pieces can also be stuck together with fabric glue.

Make as many bananas as you want because these will be your "score cards." The height tree can be used with a number of children—simply use a different colored pen for each new name so that each child's banana can be easily identified.

To attach the monkeys and bananas to the tree I sprayed the backs of the pieces with spray adhesive. This is a glue that does not permanently fix the items in place, but allows you to reposition them when you want.

# Day One

## Step 1

Using the templates on pages 72 and 73, cut out the components for the palm leaves and monkeys.

Each palm leaf requires three pieces—two sides to the leaf and the front piece.

Each monkey has one body in brown, feet and hands in red, and a fawn face.

Each banana is made of two identical crescents.

## Step 2

Assemble the monkeys. Glue the feet, hands, and face onto the main body and allow to dry.

## Step 3

Using tiny stitches, sew on eye and mouth detail with dark thread.

## Step 4

To assemble each palm leaf, machine stitch the frond section to the inside curved edge of a green felt crescent.

## Step 5

Place the right sides of the palm leaf together with the frond sandwiched in between and machine stitch all the way around, leaving a 4" (10cm) gap so that it can be turned inside out. Angle around the outer side of the crescent by cutting little "V" snips and make small snips up to the row of stitches on the inner crescent; then turn right side out. The frond piece should be hanging loose.

1

2

3

4

5

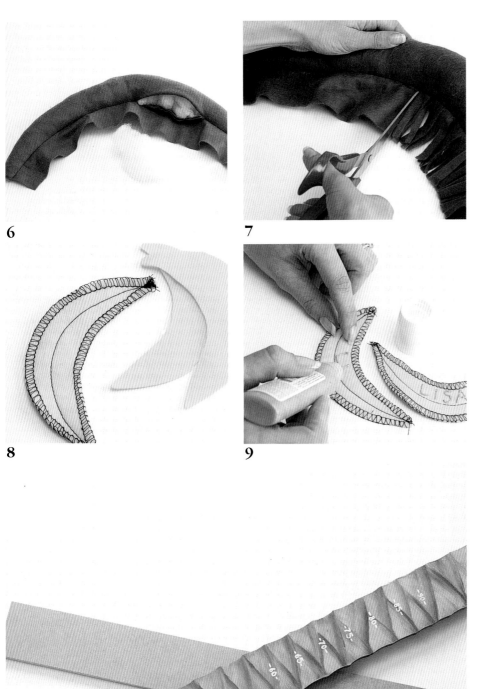

6

7

8

9

10

## Step 6
Take the 4oz (115g) batting and gently shred it up, and then stuff it into the palm leaf. You may find using the handle of a wooden spoon helpful in pushing the batting right up into the ends. When the leaf is firmly stuffed hand sew the opening.

## Step 7
Using sharp scissors cut the frond section to create a fringe effect. Repeat Steps 4–7 for the other palm leaves.

## Day Two

## Step 8
To make each banana place two yellow pieces together, then machine stitch with overlocking or zigzag stitch all the way around the edge with black thread. Add a single machine line in black thread down the center of the banana for extra effect. Repeat for the other bananas.

## Step 9
Personalize the bananas using the fabric marker. Look for a pen that can be used to create a raised, 3-D design.

## Step 10
Take the particle board trunk and use a sharp knife to gently nick out little gouges along the sides. Smooth out any rough edges with sandpaper. Paint the trunk in a deep mustard color and, when it is dry, apply a darker color to create a tree trunk effect.

Glue the tree trunk onto a wall at the desired height (above the baseboard). Measure up from the floor and mark various height measurements on the trunk. Paint them on in a contrasting color. Finally, position the leaves using small tacks.

# Rocking chair cushions and refinish

*The age-old method of rocking the baby to sleep has worked throughout the years and this chair gives you somewhere comfortable for feeding and cuddling.*

Buying and rejuvenating antique shop furniture is an increasingly popular pastime, and directly linked to this is the surge in interest in do-it-yourself decorative finishes. It is now possible to buy kits that contain all you need to create finishes such as marble, granite, verdigris, bronze, pickled, and distressed looks—anything is possible!

But you do not need to invest in a kit for the technique used here, which creates a subtle two-tone aging effect. I used two very different colors so that the distressed look would stand out, but you could choose two similar tones for a more subtle finish. The technique is simple and allows areas of the bare wood and base coat to show through the top coat. The amount of sanding that you do will dictate how much base color you see, so it is very much up to you to design the finished look of your chair.

The box cushion cover features a separate strip to make up the depth of the cushion, which is highlighted by a contrasting piping. Box cushions use blocks of foam to pad the cushion; these can be cut to size and will not lose their shape over time.

The idea of the headrest is to make it more comfortable for you when feeding your baby. It is made in exactly the same way as the seat cushion and makes the chair feel much more luxurious. (For more tips on box cushions see the Cushion-topped toy box project on page 60.)

(For more tips on box cushions see the Cushion-topped toy box project on page 60.)

## Planning your time

**DAY ONE**
**AM:** Make templates and cut out pieces for cushions; insert zippers into the depth strips and make the piping

**PM:** Machine sew seat cushion together and headrest cushion together; insert foam pads

**DAY TWO**
**AM:** Prime the chair and sand it; apply first paint color

**PM:** Sand base color and apply top color; sand top color and varnish

## Tools and materials

Fabric for cushion and headrest

2" (5cm) thick foam for inside the cushions

Two zippers (the length is the width of the cushions minus 2" (5cm))

Brown paper for making templates

Pen

Scissors

Piping cord

Approximately 1yd (1m) of contrast fabric for ties and piping

Fine-grit sandpaper

White quick-drying primer

Two contrasting colors of matte latex paint

Paintbrush

Liquid varnishing wax

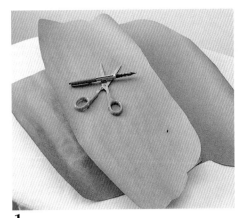

1

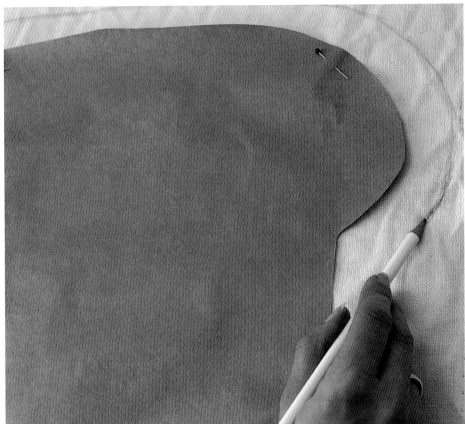

2

## Day One

### Step 1

Make the templates for the seat and head cushions out of brown paper. Lay the paper on the chair and draw the exact shape required, then cut out.

### Step 2

Draw around the template, on the wrong side of the fabric, with a ¾" (2cm) seam allowance all around. Fold the fabric double, to obtain two of each piece. Then cut them out.

### Step 3

The seat and head cushions are made in the same way.

Cut out the fabric for the depth of the cushions. Take the depth of the foam, 2" (5cm), plus ½" (1.5cm) seam allowance each side, making it 3" (8cm) deep; the length will go all around the sides and front of the cushion. Cut the back depth separately. Take the foam depth, 2" (5cm), and divide this in two, 1" (2.5cm), then add 1¼" (3cm) seam allowance on each side. Cut two pieces 2¼" (5.5cm) deep and as long as the width of the back of the cushion plus ¾" (2cm) for seam allowances. Machine stitch the zipper into the two back depth pieces, joining them together, and then machine stitch one end of this piece to the rest of the depth piece.

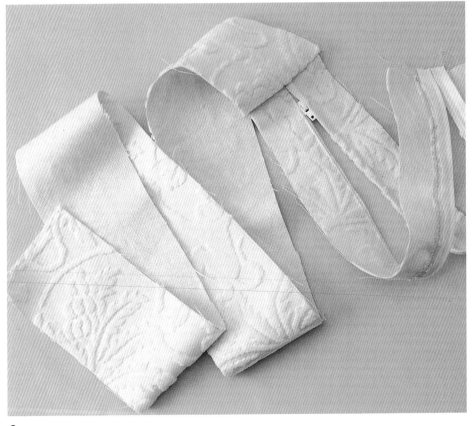

3

4

5

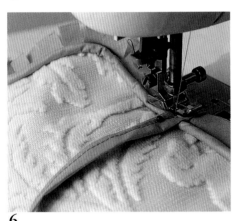

6

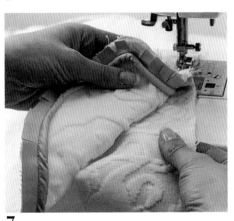

7

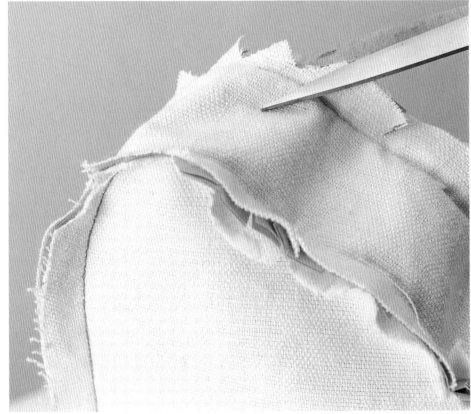

8

## Step 4

To make piping it is important that you always cut the fabric strips on the bias. Cut them as long as possible and about 2" (5cm) wide. Place the piping cord in the center of the fabric strip and machine stitch the two edges together, with a zipper foot, close to the piping cord.

## Step 5

Pin the piping around the top and bottom piece of the cushion fabric and machine stitch in place. When sewing around corners the piping will sit better if you snip the fabric up to the seam.

## Step 6

Cut and make the ties. You will need four on each cushion. To make a tie, cut a piece of fabric 2x16" (5x40cm), fold both long edges into the center, and press. Then fold the whole length in half again and machine stitch down the edges. Machine two of these, equally spaced across the back, onto the rear of the cushion; repeat for both the top and bottom piece of the cushion.

## Step 7

Starting with the zippered piece centrally placed at the back, pin the depth strip to the top cushion piece along the existing seam line of where the piping was sewn, and then machine stitch. Open the zipper, pin, and machine sew the bottom cushion piece to the remaining side of the depth strip.

## Step 8

Angle all the corners by cutting little "V" snips and clip into the seam allowance wherever there are any bends.

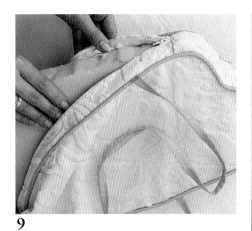

9

## Step 9

Cut a piece of foam to size from the original paper templates for both the seat cushion and head pad. Insert into the cushion covers.

## Day Two

## Step 10

Apply a coat of quick-drying primer to the bare wood chair and allow to dry. When this is completely dry, sand the chair lightly and then wipe down to remove all traces of dust.

## Step 11

Apply a coat of paint of your chosen base color. In this case I used a lime-green color. Paint the whole chair and then let it dry completely.

### *Box cushions*

Box cushion covers are different from other cushion covers because they have a separate strip that makes up the depth of the cushion. Box cushions also use blocks of foam to pad the cushion, making for a sharper look, especially where piping has been used.

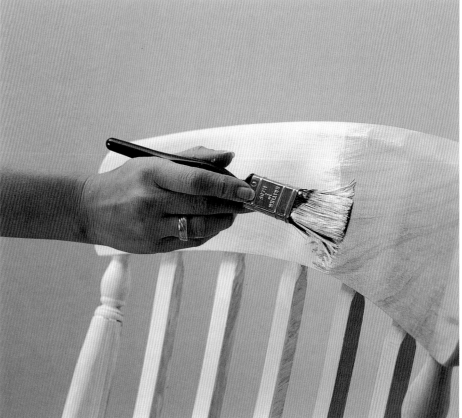

10

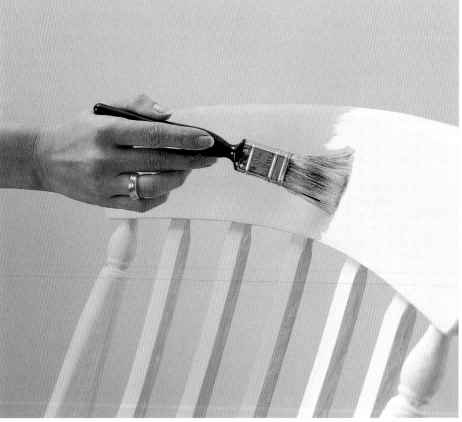

11

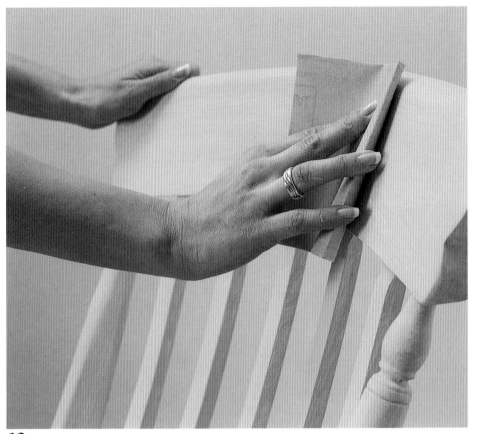

**12**

**14**

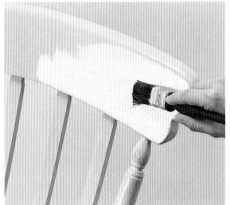

**15**

**13**

### Step 12
Lightly sand the chair again to give a smooth finish, and using a damp sponge, wipe over it to remove all traces of dust.

### Step 13
Paint on the top coat, in this case lilac, and allow to dry.

### Step 14
The final sanding process needs a little more thought! Sand in the direction of the grain, especially along the edges and around joints to reveal the base color of lime green. Continue sanding until you are happy with the distressed look. Wipe the chair down well after sanding to remove all dust.

### Step 15
The final coat is a layer of varnishing wax. Allow to dry and then buff the

# Stenciled wall design

*This stenciled wall continues the design elements in the curtain fabric all over the room. Brightly colored fruits and flowers are appealing to all ages of children.*

It is easy to paint a wall in one solid color, but the end result can be rather boring. If you follow this project, however, you will discover that painting stripes is a cinch. You do not need to paint all four walls in the room with stripes; just two striped walls would look equally impressive.

If you have never attempted to stencil, here is your opportunity. Do not be limited by store-bought designs—make your own stencil, it is easy! This will open up a whole range of possibilities for you. I took inspiration from this fun fruit and floral curtain fabric. The fruits were simple shapes and could easily be traced onto acetate to create a stencil. These were then stenciled above a chair rail.

A chair rail is a piece of decorative molding that is fixed onto the wall at waist height—we made ours out of lengths of shaped particle board, which were painted to look like orange segments. Below the chair rail I painted narrow stripes, and when they were dry I stuck on some flowerpots that I cut out of the coordinating wallpaper border.

I followed the orange segment theme through by creating a cornice for the window out of a piece of particle board cut into a semicircle and then painted.

Finishing touches included tiebacks that feature little padded pineapples and a selection of cushions all appliquéd with an assortment of fruit. These designs were all simply cut out of the curtain fabric. So, whether you are going to buy some new fabric for this project or use existing curtains, inspect your material; it could provide the elements for the theme you choose.

## Day One

### Step 1

Place a sheet of acetate over the design that you want to turn into a stencil. Trace the design with an acetate pen, making sure that you draw all the dividing lines where colors change. If the designs that you want to trace need enlarging or reducing, simply copy them onto tracing paper first and use a photocopier to get them to your desired size, then trace them onto the acetate sheets.

### Step 2

Before you start cutting be sure that the design you have drawn will not fall apart when it is cut. Cut out your stencils on a cutting mat, using a craft knife.

### Step 3

Decorate the shaped, particle board decorative trim. I took my inspiration from the fabric and painted segments of orange onto each semicircle of the trim. After the base coat of orange paint has dried, add the white detail lines. Then use some raw umber acrylic paint to fill in the segment details.

### Step 4

To create the striped effect under the chair rail, use a pencil and level to mark the wall 43¼" (110cm) high and draw a stripe every 3" (8cm). Use the level to make sure that all the vertical lines are parallel.

### Step 5

Use the pencil line as a guide to place the center of the roller over, as it will cover the pencil mark. Wrap a rubber band around each end of the roller. This results in an exaggerated wiggly line. Load the roller with paint from the paint tray, and placing it centrally over a pencil mark, slowly paint down the line. Continue painting the lines until you have completed the area.

1

2

3

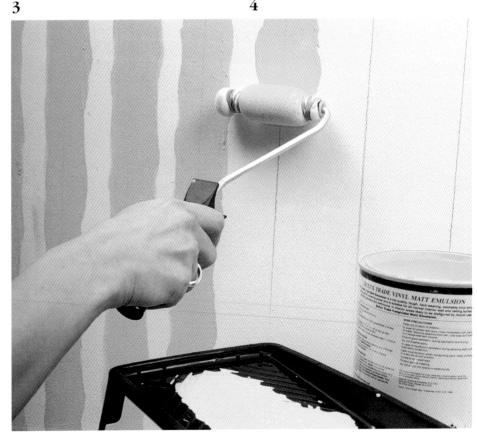

4

5

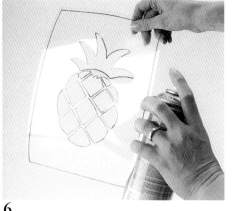

6

7

8

9

10

11

## Day Two

### Step 6
Apply a light, even coat of spray adhesive onto the back of the stencil and position it on the wall.

### Step 7
Take the stencil brush and dip it into a little paint and then wipe off the excess on a piece of paper towel. The brush should be almost dry before you start stenciling.

### Step 8
Using a gentle stabbing motion, apply the paint to the wall. Repeat until the stencil is complete, then gently peel off the stencil. Use a fine artist's brush to add any detail lines.

### Step 9
If the fabric has a coordinating wallpaper or border, you can cut out details from it to stick on the bottom half of the wall.

### Step 10
Take the caulking gun of nail-strength adhesive and apply a line of it to the back of the particle board trim. Fix the trim onto the wall above the stripes to create the chair rail.

### Step 11
Finish the wall by sticking the wallpaper cutouts on the striped area.

# Lampshades

*These lampshades turn a nursery light into something really different. Fluffy sheep will help your baby go to sleep or roses will set a soft, gentle scene.*

Lighting is important in a nursery and it is helpful to have at least a couple of different light sources to create different moods. If you are awakened at 3 A.M. you certainly will not want to switch the main light on, and the option of a subtle table night light creates a soft attractive glow.

Most lampshades that you can buy are very plain, but these make ideal canvases on which to let loose your imagination. You can also give a makeover treatment to existing lampshades that you may have hanging from central lights or sitting on a lampbase. Look around the room in which you want to create your new-look shade and see if anything inspires you as a basis for a design. If nothing impresses you, flip through a few baby books where you will be bombarded with all sorts of images that could be perfect for this project.

I loved the idea of decorating a lampshade with jumping sheep, cute and fluffy. The white furry fabric that I found in the craft department of a fabric store is perfect for the sheep body, while fine feather trim bought by the length gives a great finishing touch.

If you want a more romantic look for the nursery, how about a lampshade smothered with roses of all shapes and sizes? Ready-made roses are available in stores and look great mixed with the larger homemade variety.

## Planning your time

**DAY ONE**

AM: Attach eyelets onto shade; spray shade and cut out sheep shapes

PM: Stick on sheep bodies; add top and bottom trims

**DAY TWO**

AM: Make up ribbon roses and sew them onto shade

PM: Glue on ready-made roses and glue on fringe

## Tools and materials

Plain lampshade

Strong adhesive glue

Scissors

For the sheep lampshade:
Eyelet hole punch and metal eyelets

Fabric marker

Spray paint in bright green

Black yarn
(for sheep's legs)

Small piece of black felt
(for sheep's head)

White fluffy fabric
(for sheep's body)

1yd (1m) of fluffy white trim
(for around top and bottom of shade)

Approximately 1yd (1m) of green narrow ribbon

Approximately ½yd (500cm) of pink narrow ribbon

For the rose lampshade:
20" (50cm) of wired ribbon
(for each big rose)

Assortment of miniature, ready-made roses

Needle and cotton thread

Fringe—enough to go around the base of the shade

# "Counting sheep" lampshade

## Step 1
Take a plain lampshade and mark around the top and bottom edges where the eyelet holes are to be punched; I marked them every 1¼" (3cm). Use a punch to make the holes and insert the metal eyelets all around the top and base of the lampshade.

## Step 2
Spray the lampshade grass green. Do this in a well-ventilated area. Allow to dry for a few hours.

## Step 3
Using the templates on page 71, cut out a sheep's body from fluffy white fabric, and a sheep's head from black felt. Cut out as many sheep as you can fit around the frame. Then cut pieces of black yarn 1¼" (3cm) long for each leg (four per sheep!).

## Step 4
Glue the sheep onto the lampshade. Put the body in place first, then the head and legs. Allow to dry. Make sure all edges adhere to the shade. Using a fabric marker, draw on two little eyes to complete the sheep's face.

## Step 5
Attach fluffy white trim around the top and bottom of the shade. Secure it with ribbon threaded in and out of the eyelet holes. Secure the ends of the ribbon with a bow.

### Using lights safely
It is advisable to use a low-watt lightbulb in lights that have had decorations attached to them.

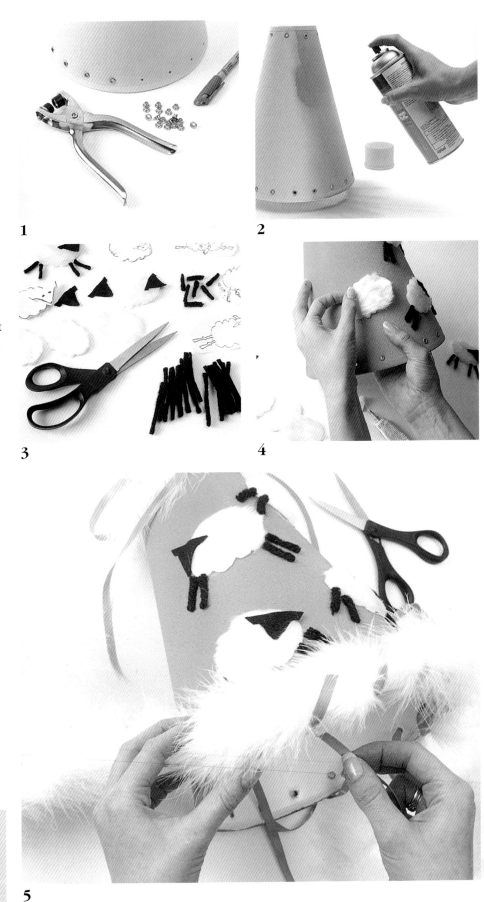

1

2

3

4

5

# "Roses grow on you" lampshade

## Step 1
To make each wired rose you need 20" (50cm) of wired ribbon. Gently gather a piece of ribbon by pulling the wire and scrunching the ribbon. Then fold one end over and secure it with some hand-sewn stitches, using a needle and a fairly long cotton thread.

## Step 2
Continue to roll the ribbon around, sewing it at the base to hold the rose together. Keep folding the ribbon until you reach the end and then fold that end in, securing it with a stitch.

## Step 3
Using the same needle and piece of thread, sew the rose directly onto the lampshade so that it is held securely in place. Make all the other roses and sew them all over the lampshade until it is evenly covered.

## Step 4
Using the glue, apply a little to the back of the miniature roses and stick them on in between the larger ones, until the shade has a good covering of roses.

## Step 5
Apply some glue all the way around the base of the shade and stick on the fringe. Allow to dry for a few hours.

1

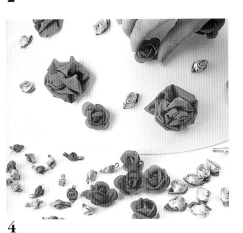

2

3

4

5

### Dyeing fringe

If you cannot find fringe in the exact color that you require, try dyeing it! As long as you buy natural cotton fringe, it can be dyed using a cold-water dye.

# Duck-hooded towel

*Warm and practical, this duck-hooded towel will help make bath time fun for both you and your baby. Older children will enjoy having one of these character towels too.*

### Planning your time

**DAY ONE**
**AM:** Cut out the pieces and machine the hooded section and bill together

**PM:** Sew on the eyes

**DAY TWO**
**AM:** Sew on the feet; attach the hooded section to the main body; hem and top stitch it

### Tools and materials

**1yd (1m) of yellow terry cloth, or a yellow bath towel**

**10" (25cm) of orange terry cloth, or an orange hand towel**

**6" (15cm) of plain black terry cloth**

**6" (15cm) of plain white terry cloth**

**Scissors**

Whereas some babies seem to revel in warm water and find it a real pleasure to be bathed, others object strongly to being undressed and dipped in water. So in order to encourage them to associate the whole experience with fun, I have made a hooded bath wrap with the face of a duck on it. The towel can be wrapped around the baby as soon as he or she is taken out of the bath.

All the pieces are made from terry cloth, so the whole wrap can be treated like a normal towel and thrown in the washing machine when dirty. I used embossed terry cloth for the main parts, which gave the duck an overall textured finish.

Terry cloth is very easy to work with but does need to be hemmed to keep it from fraying. Special products to prevent fraying are available from craft shops and these can be painted onto the back of the fabric—however, the fabric must be thoroughly dry again before you cut it out.

A good tip for basic appliqué is to join the cutout motifs to the background fabric with fusible webbing. I used this method for the eyes in this project. This will eliminate the problem of any motifs becoming distorted when machine sewed on. Alternately, you could use fabric glue. Fix the cutout motifs in place with it, once more allowing it to dry thoroughly before machine zigzagging around the shapes.

You should be able to set the zigzag controls on your sewing machine in various ways to produce a stitch that covers the cut edge of an appliqué motif. A narrow, open zigzag allows some of the fabric to show through while a wide, closely set satin stitch is dense enough to hide the edge completely. Try experimenting first on a scrap of fabric until you are happy with the results.

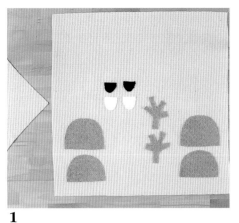

1

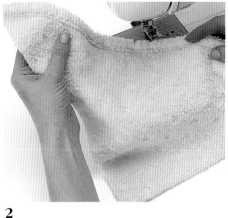

2

3

## Day One

### Step 1

Cut out all the pieces.

The main body measures 37½x37½" (95x95cm).

The triangular hood has two equal sides of 14" (36cm) at right angles to each other.

Use the templates on page 74. Enlarge them to the right size and cut two large beak pieces, two smaller beak pieces, two whites of eyes, two black pupils, and two feet.

### Step 2

Hem the triangular hood section along its longest side by turning in a small seam. Hem the main body of the duck all the way around the edge.

### Step 3

Machine sew the two pieces of each beak together. Place the smaller beak piece onto the large beak piece, right sides together and with the curved edges meeting. Machine stitch them together around the curved edge and then angle the beak by cutting little "V" snips all the way around the curve. Then turn it right side out. Repeat this for the other beak piece.

4

### Step 4

Machine sew the beaks to the hood. Take the hood section and pin one beak to the top side of the hood (that is, the right side of the hood fabric) and one beak to the bottom side of the hood (that is, the wrong side of the hood fabric). Machine stitch in place along the slightly larger beak edge.

### Terry cloth or towels

When buying terry cloth it is also worth having a look in the towel department. It may be less expensive, especially on sale, to buy a couple of towels and flannels to make the duck.

**5**

**6**

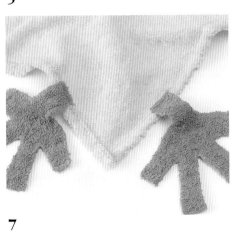

**7**

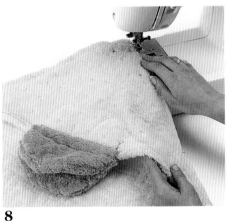

**8**

**9**

## Step 5

Fold the beaks over so that they are sitting on top of each other and sew another row of machine stitches to secure the beaks together. You should do this over the original machine row that holds the beaks to the hoods.

## Step 6

Appliqué the blacks of the eyes onto the white pieces and then appliqué the whites of the eyes onto the hood. Pin them very close to the beak and make sure they are in the right position before machine stitching them.

## Day Two

### Step 7

Zigzag stitch all the way around the feet to keep them from fraying, and then machine sew them onto the bottom corner of the towel.

### Step 8

Now pin the hood onto the main body. Place the right sides together and position it in the top corner—the one that is diagonally opposite the corner where the feet have been attached. Machine stitch around the two outside edges. Turn the hood right side out.

### Step 9

Machine sew a row of top stitches around the two outside edges of the hood, for a professional touch.

> ## *Finishing raw edges*
>
> When the appliqué eye pieces are pinned in place, machine sew in zigzag stitch all the way around each piece to finish the edges. Make sure that all rough edges are well stitched down.

# Noah's ark wall frieze

*Noah's ark all around the nursery walls will give your baby plenty to look at. Animal shapes are easy to make out of salt dough and the variety of options is endless.*

Creating a 3-D frieze on the nursery wall can provide some colorful action with which to attract your baby's attention. The animals in this project were made out of salt dough. Salt dough has been a worldwide art form for centuries, and interpretations of the craft are found in places as far apart as Mexico and Scandinavia. In some parts of Europe it is an age-old tradition to make Christmas decorations and gifts from salt dough.

Salt dough is fun to work with and is also relatively inexpensive, salt and flour being the main ingredients. Once rolled out, it can be treated like normal cookie dough. I used cookie cutters to make the shapes of the animals, but if you master handling the dough and feel adventurous you can try your luck with freehand shapes. Experiment with different kitchen utensils too! Dough put through a garlic press creates a mass of fine spaghetti-like pieces. You could imprint the dough with a mesh strainer for a textured finish. You can also color the dough with food dyes, spices, and coffee.

Salt dough is a fun technique that you can use to create an endless source of designs. Once varnished, your animals will last a lifetime. However, it is worth noting not to place them near direct heat, such as a radiator, and, to keep them looking clean, remember to dust them once in a while.

The wallpaper waves were cut using a craft knife immediately after the paper was pasted to the wall (that is, before it had adhered properly). You could also make a stencil of a wave out of cardboard. Lightly pencil a shallow curving line on the wall from one side to the other. Use this as a guide to position the stencils.

## Day One

### Step 1

Using the templates on page 75 and 76, enlarge them until you are satisfied with the size. Cut the three pieces that make the ark's body out of corrugated cardboard. The two window frames are simply hollowed-out squares and the door frame is an arch.

### Step 2

Using latex paint, add some detailing to the ark. I painted spots around the window and door, large spots on the ark's base, and a hint of green on the roof. Allow to dry. Then stick the door frame and window frames to the middle piece of the ark.

### Step 3

Apply some glue to the back of the ark and attach all the pieces to the wall. I continued the wave effect of the wallpaper over the ark's base using blue latex paint.

### Step 4

Make up the salt dough mixture. The basic recipe is: 2 cups of flour to 1 cup of salt and 1 cup of water. Mix the flour and salt together and slowly add the water until a dough consistency is formed. You may find that you do not need to add all the water or that you may need a drop more. Either way, knead the dough well for five minutes and allow to stand for 20 minutes, in a plastic bag, before working on it.

### Step 5

Roll out the dough on a lightly floured board to about ½" (1cm) thick, and using the cookie cutters, cut out two of each animal. Place them on a lightly greased baking sheet and bake them in a low oven, 100°F (50°C), for 10 hours. Turn the animals over halfway through the baking process.

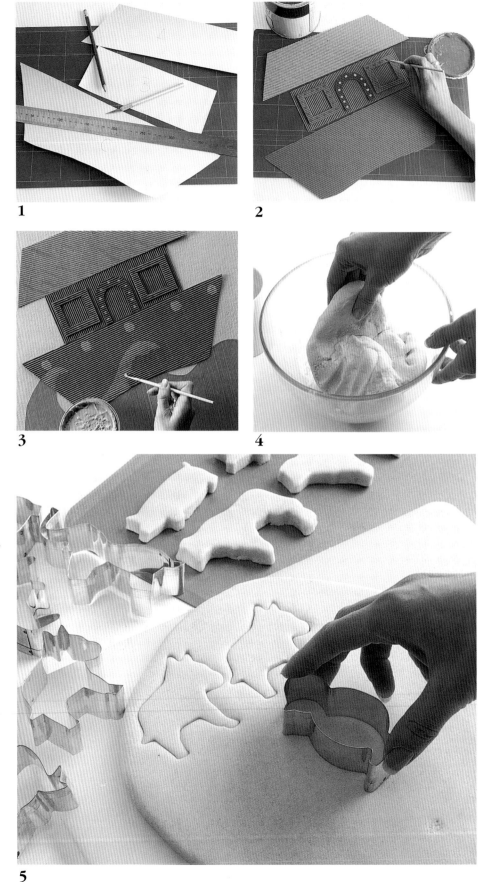

1

2

3

4

5

6

7

8

9

10

11

## Step 6
The salt dough animals will turn
golden brown while baking. Tap them
to check if they are ready—they will
sound hollow. If air bubbles form on
their surface during baking, simply
pierce them and press them flat and
turn the oven temperature down. After
removing them from the oven, allow
the shapes to cool.

## Day Two

### Step 7
Paint each animal with white latex
paint and allow to dry thoroughly.

### Step 8
Paint the animals in appropriate colors,
making sure to paint their edges as
well. Let them dry.

### Step 9
Using contrasting colors, paint in any
features to help make the animals more
identifiable. Let them dry.

### Step 10
To protect the animals, give them a
coat of spray polyurethane matte
varnish. Work in a well-ventilated area.

### Step 11
Glue the animals, two by two, to the
wall. Use masking tape to hold the
pairs in place until the glue has set.

# Cushion-topped toy box

*This toy box will comfortably keep a large collection of toys safe, clean, and out of the way. As well as giving you much-needed storage, it is an extra place to sit.*

## Tools and materials

Ready-made toy box with lid

5' (1.5m) of fabric

2" (5cm) thick foam
to fit top of box

Scissors

Zipper the length of the cushion
minus 2" (5cm)

1yd (1m) of fabric for
making piping

Piping cord

1yd (1m) of ¼" (5mm) wide
flat elastic

Decorative pom-poms
or tassels (optional)

Nurseries are often bursting with soft toys that have been amassed over the years. If you do not have the heart to get rid of some of them, a large toy box makes an ideal new home for them. If your nursery is tight on space, however, you might think twice about introducing another large item of furniture into the room. So why not give it a dual purpose and transform it into a cushioned bench seat?

A box-seat cushion padded with deep foam makes a comfortable and easy-to-clean seat. The advantage of using foam is that the cushion will keep its shape. To make it easy to remove the cover, I recommend that you insert a full-length zipper along the back-side depth.

Foam is available in sheets or blocks and in a variety of qualities or grades. It is easy to cut; simply lay the seat pattern on it and draw an outline on the foam with a felt tip pen. Cut the foam to size with a sharp kitchen knife or an electric carving knife. It is essential to make sure that the label on the foam indicates it is flame retardant.

The elastic that is machined onto the underside of the cushion will hold it in place, especially if the lid of the box is to be lifted frequently.

A variety of easy-to-apply trims can be used to decorate cushions. When used with imagination, these can add a stylish and individual finish. This project explains in detail how to make piping and to use it with a fun zigzag edging. For the finishing touch, I used coordinating pom-poms.

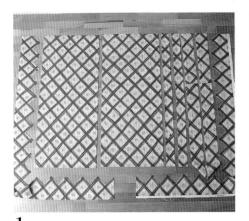

1

2

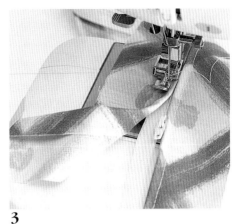

3

## Day One

### Step 1

Measure the width and length of the box and add 1¼" (3cm). Cut out two pieces of fabric this size for the top and bottom pieces of the cushion. Measure the front length and add to it the two side lengths, then add 1¼" (3cm) seam allowance for overall length. Cut a strip of fabric the total length by 2" (5cm) deep.

Cut out two strips for the back length of the cushion, which will have the zipper sewn into them. These should be the length of the toy box plus 1¼" (3cm) by 2¼" (5.5cm) deep (this is the depth of the foam 2" [5cm], divided by 2 to give 1" [2.5cm], with 1¼" [3cm] seam allowance added). For the flag-edged trim, cut out two strips the same length as the other long side strips by whatever depth you want the flags to be. (The flags do not continue around the back of the box.)

### Step 2

Machine stitch the two strips of flag-edged trim together. Place the right sides of the fabric together and machine stitch along the zigzag edge. Trim and angle each point. Turn the trim right side out, and press it.

4

### Step 3

Machine stitch the zipper into the back two sections. Fold over ⅝" (1.5cm) on one side of each back strip and press with a warm iron. Then, using a zipper foot on your sewing machine, sew the zipper onto each side of the back sections. Join this strip onto the end of the very long strip, thus making a strip that should reach all the way around the cushion.

### Step 4

Make the piping. Cut lengths of fabric on the bias, 2" (5cm) wide and as long as possible. Machine stitch the strips together, again on the bias, to make a very long piece. Place piping cord in the center and fold the fabric lengthwise, wrong sides together. Machine stitch the two edges with a zipper foot, close to the cord, but not through it! Make enough piping to go around the edge of the cushion twice.

# Day Two

## Step 5

Take the bottom piece of fabric for the cushion and machine stitch on a piece of elastic 4" (10cm) in from the edge on each end and on the right side of the fabric. Just secure each end of the elastic onto the edges. The length of elastic needs to be 3¼" (8cm) less than the width of the fabric. It is this elastic on each end that will hold the cushion onto the lid of the toy box. Then pin on the flag-edged trim, still working on the right side of the fabric. Start at the back corner and work your way up the first side, across the front, and then down the other side. Angling the corners while you are pinning the trim on will help it to sit comfortably. Then machine stitch the trim on.

## Step 6

Still working on the bottom piece of the cushion, and on the right side of the fabric, pin on the piping. This will go around the whole cushion. Again, angle each corner for a smooth curve. Then machine sew the piping in place.

## Step 7

Take the top piece of fabric and pin on the remaining piping, once more cutting off the fabric at the corners. Try using the existing stitch line on the piping as a guide for when you sew the next row of stitches.

## Step 8

Still working on the top piece of fabric, pin on the strip with the zipper. Start by pinning the zippered piece centrally across the back side of the fabric and then work your way around until you reach the back again. Again, angle the corners for a smooth curve. Make sure that you pin right under the piping on the outer edge so that when you machine stitch it on, the piping will stand up.

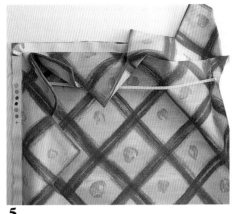

5

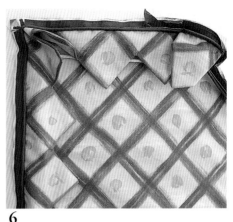

6

7

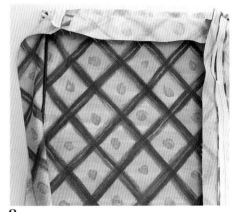

8

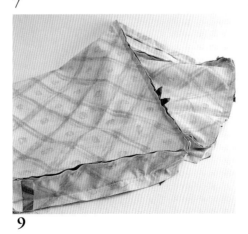

9

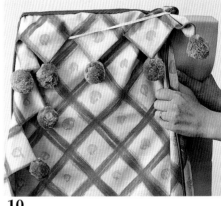

10

## Step 9

Working on the wrong side of the fabric, pin the top and bottom pieces of the cushion together; open the zipper to help you reach the inside of the cushion. Machine stitch all the way around the edge. The cushion should now be completed but inside out. Angle all the corners and then turn right side out. Hand sew on any extra trim securely.

## Step 10

Take the piece of foam, put it inside the cushion cover, and zip it up. Make sure that the fabric and trim is lying neatly before attaching the cushion to the lid of the toy box with the elastic strips.

# Cradle makeover

*Here is a special cradle for a special baby! An ordinary crib becomes a work of art with the application of a color wash and carefully planned découpage.*

**Planning your time**

**DAY ONE**
AM: Color wash the cradle;
cut out paper motifs

PM: Stick the paper motifs
onto the cradle and varnish them

**DAY TWO**
AM: Sand the cradle and
apply more varnish

PM: Apply the gilding wax,
sand, and apply another
coat of varnish

**Tools and materials**

Sanding block and
fine-grit sandpaper

Small can of white latex paint

Two small cans of colored
latex paint

Bath sponge

Plastic bucket for mixing paint

Paintbrush

Wrapping paper

Craft knife and cutting mat

Double-sided tape

All-purpose strong adhesive

One can of quick-drying
satin varnish

Small jar of gilding wax

Cloth for buffing

The découpage technique that I used on this cradle dates back to the seventeenth century! The French word "découpage" means "cutting out" and gives its name to the art of decorating objects with cutout paper motifs. These paper pieces are carefully arranged, glued to the surface, and then covered with layers of varnish so that the edges of the paper are invisible.

Découpage can be used to good effect on many objects. While items decorated in this way look as if they are the work of a talented artist, in fact the skill involved is easily acquired by anyone with a little patience.

Look around for a wide source of motifs. These can come from greeting cards, wrapping paper, postcards, or even scraps of wallpaper. Making a successful arrangement of your chosen images is the most important part of découpage. That is why it is advisable to plan the position of your images using double-sided tape first.

Traditionally, from 15 to 20 coats of varnish were normally applied, each coat being gently rubbed down with sandpaper. I am of the opinion that the more coats, the better, but if you only have time to apply five or six layers of varnish this should be adequate. However, if you are going to use this technique on a surface that may get substantial wear, then I would recommend applying considerably more.

The paint technique used in this project is color washing. It is very easy to mix up and apply a color wash, but first make sure that the paint you are using is water based since the color wash is made by mixing paint with water. You will find with this technique that a little paint goes a long way, so you can buy small cans of paints.

1

## Day One

### Step 1

Strip down the cradle to its bare wood and sand it well for a smooth finish. The technique of color washing requires the wood to be clean and all the grain and knots to be visible. Wipe down the cradle with a damp cloth to remove any dust.

### Step 2

Mix the color wash in a plastic paint bucket. Color wash is simply a watered-down matte latex paint. When latex paint is watered down it creates an opaque solution that, when applied, allows the wood grain to show through. The recipe for a color wash is variable, but I recommend approximately 1 part latex to 5 parts water. Experiment with the mix until you have the desired finish. Make sure that you thoroughly mix the paint into the water for an even finish.

### Step 3

Dip the sponge into the color wash and gently squeeze out the excess. Using a fluid hand movement, rub the sponge over the cradle, working in the direction of the wood grain. Work very quickly because the paint dries quickly. Build up the coverage until you have the depth of color you wish.

2

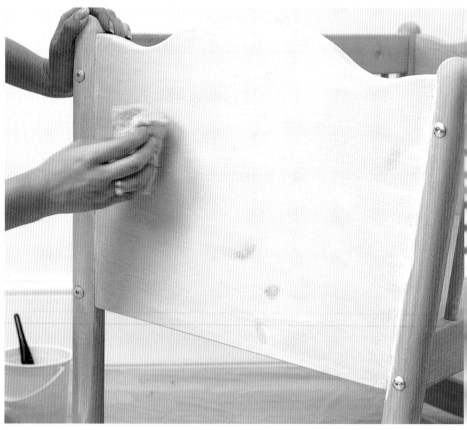

3

4

5

6

7

## Step 4

Mix a color wash in the other colors that you have chosen and then use these colors to highlight any interesting features on the cradle, such as the side rails. Because the color wash is thin and runny you only need a very small amount on the brush or sponge to work with.

## Step 5

Figure out how many designs you will need to cover the cradle and cut them out of wrapping paper using a craft knife. Pay particular attention to any sharp corners or grooves that need careful cutting around.

## Step 6

Using double-sided tape, arrange the cutouts on the cradle in a design that you like. Doing this gives you an opportunity to play around with the final placement of the cutouts. For child safety reasons, only apply the design to the outside of the cradle.

## Step 7

When you are happy with the position of the cutouts, apply some glue over the back of each piece and carefully glue in place. Allow to dry properly.

### *Choosing nontoxic paints*

Before beginning to paint any furniture that a baby might chew on it is vital that you check that the paints and materials that you will be using are nontoxic and safe for babies. There are many products available nowadays that fall into this category, so you will not be limited in your choice of colors and finishes.

**8**

### Step 8

Apply a coat of varnish over the découpage to seal it. Do not apply too thick of a coat; this is the first of five coats to be applied. Allow the varnish to dry.

### Day Two

### Step 9

In between each coat of varnish use fine-grit sandpaper to gently sand the surface. Wipe off all the dust in preparation for the next coat.

### Step 10

Use gilding wax to highlight the design of the cradle. Apply it by dipping the cloth into the can and rubbing a little of the wax over the cradle edges.

**9**

## *Preparing your furniture*

Thorough preparation and groundwork are the keys to good results time and time again. So make sure that you set time aside for sanding and preparing your furniture before starting to decorate.

**10**

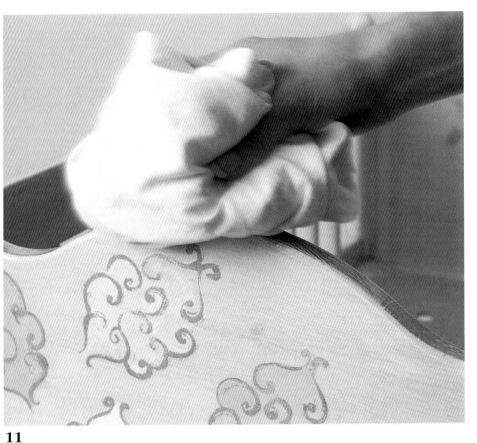

**11**

**13**

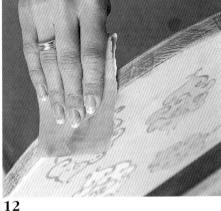

**12**

### Step 11
Using a soft cloth, gently buff the areas where you have applied the gilding wax.

### Step 12
If you wish to create a worn and softer look to the finish, gently sand back the gilding wax.

### Step 13
Finally, apply a couple of coats of varnish to the gilded areas to seal them in, remembering to gently sand down in between each coat.

### *Appropriate finishes*

Color washing is only useful if you are working on bare wood. If you have a plastic-coated crib or you do not want to strip a piece of furniture down to bare wood then you can apply a solid paint finish. Simply sand the surface and prime it with the appropriate primer and it is ready for whatever finish you wish.

# Templates

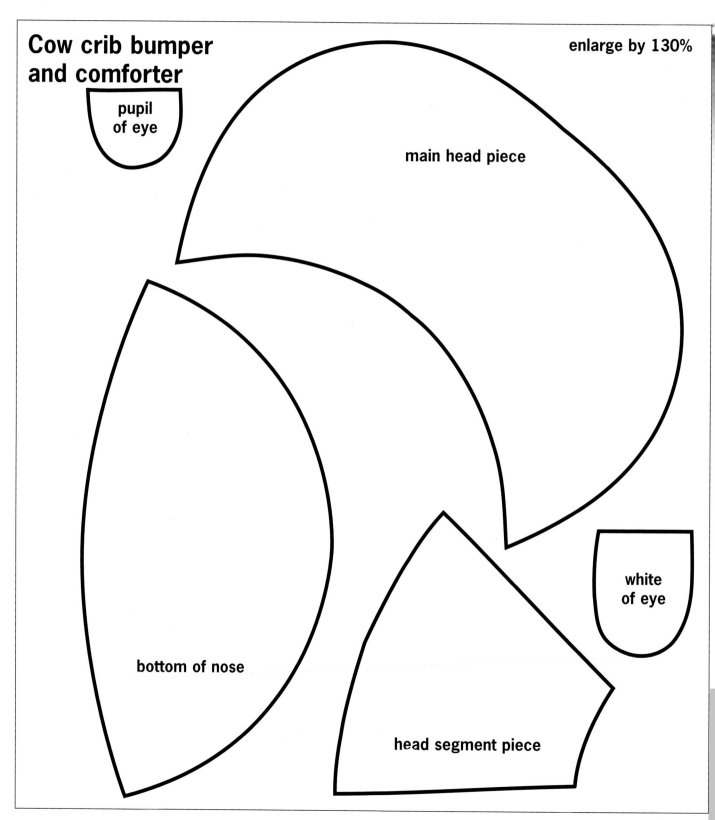

**Cow crib bumper and comforter**

enlarge by 130%

pupil of eye

main head piece

bottom of nose

white of eye

head segment piece

# Templates

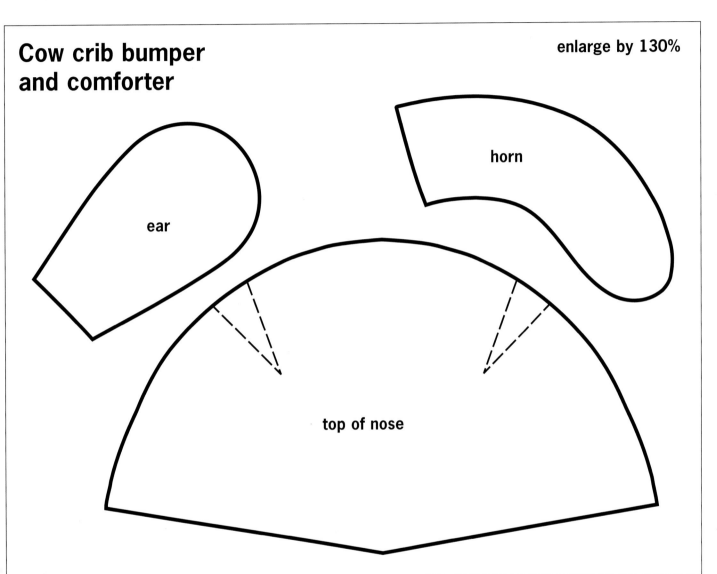

**Cow crib bumper
and comforter**

enlarge by 130%

horn

ear

top of nose

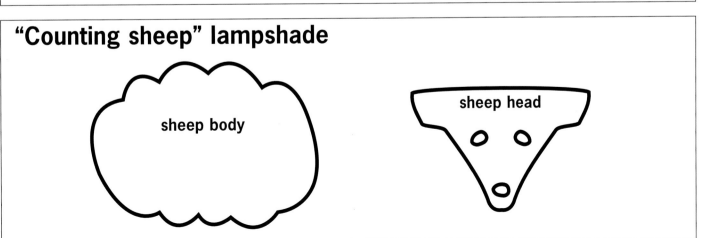

## "Counting sheep" lampshade

sheep body

sheep head

# Templates

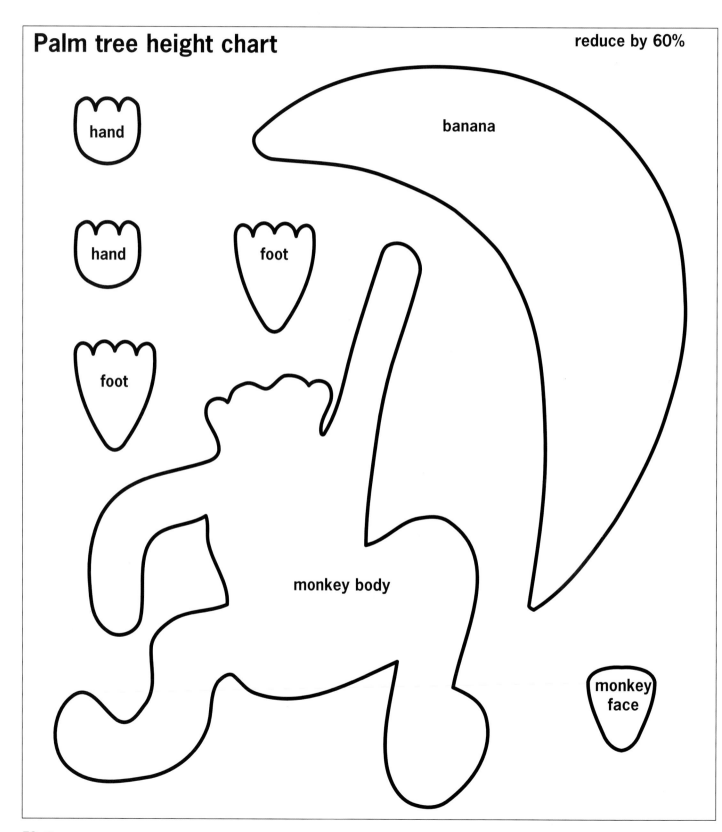

**Palm tree height chart**

reduce by 60%

hand

hand

foot

foot

banana

monkey body

monkey face

# Templates

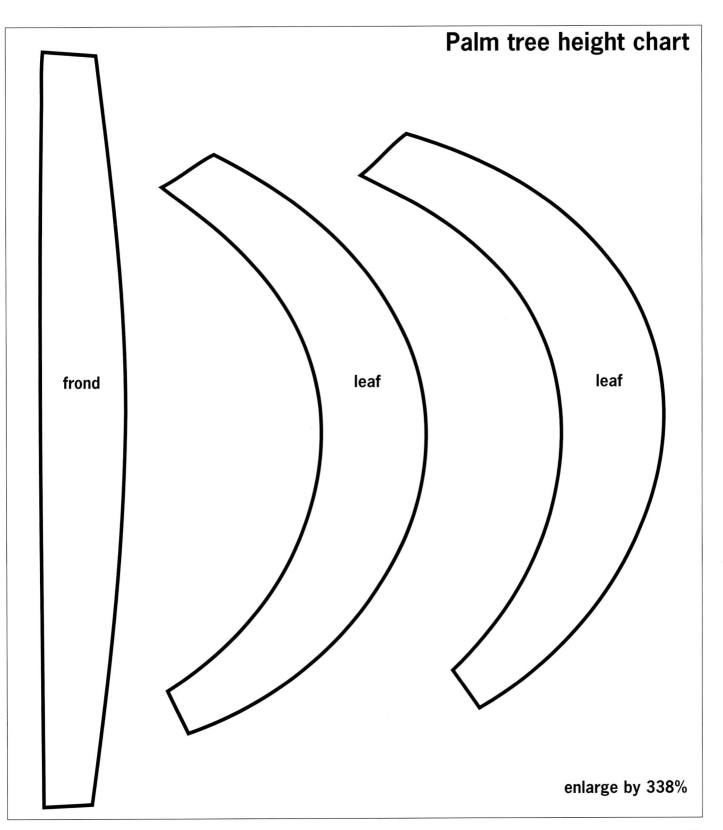

**Palm tree height chart**

frond

leaf

leaf

**enlarge by 338%**

# Templates

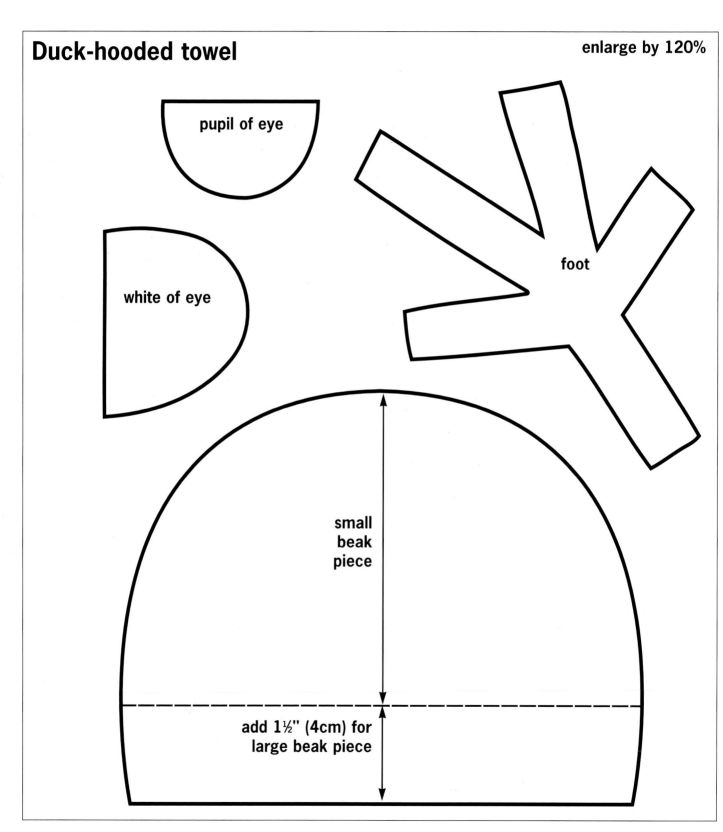

**Duck-hooded towel**

enlarge by 120%

pupil of eye

white of eye

foot

small beak piece

add 1½" (4cm) for large beak piece

# Templates

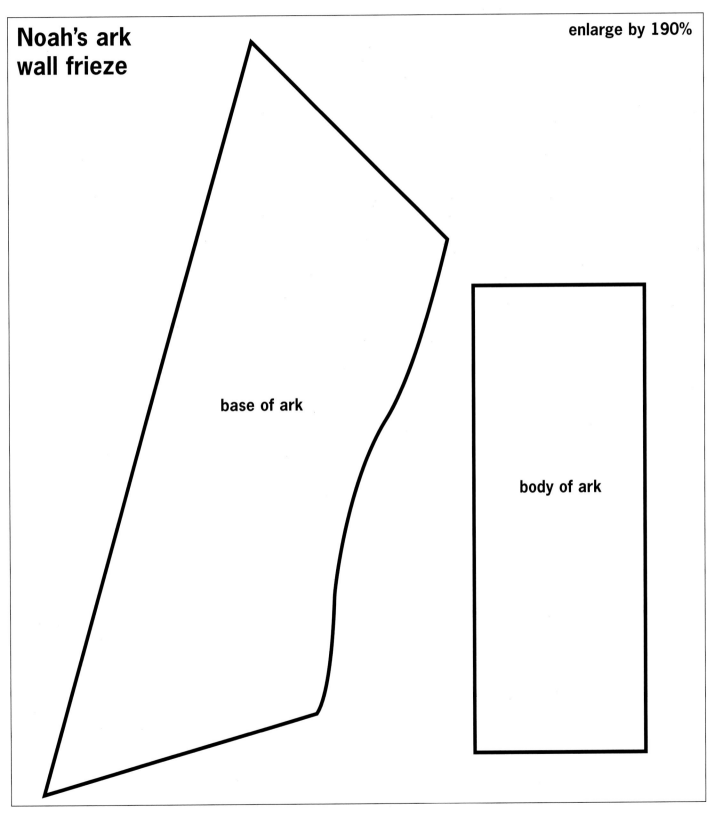

**Noah's ark
wall frieze**

enlarge by 190%

base of ark

body of ark

# Templates

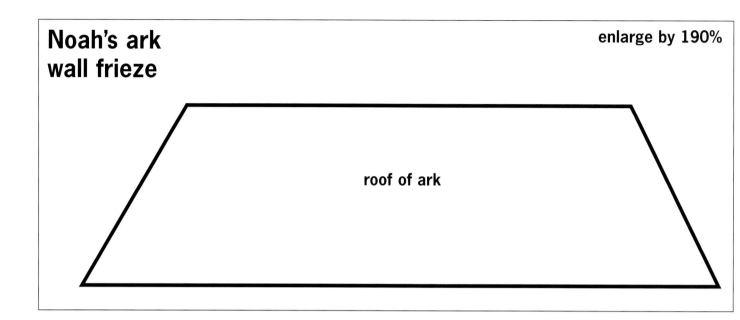

**Noah's ark wall frieze**

enlarge by 190%

roof of ark

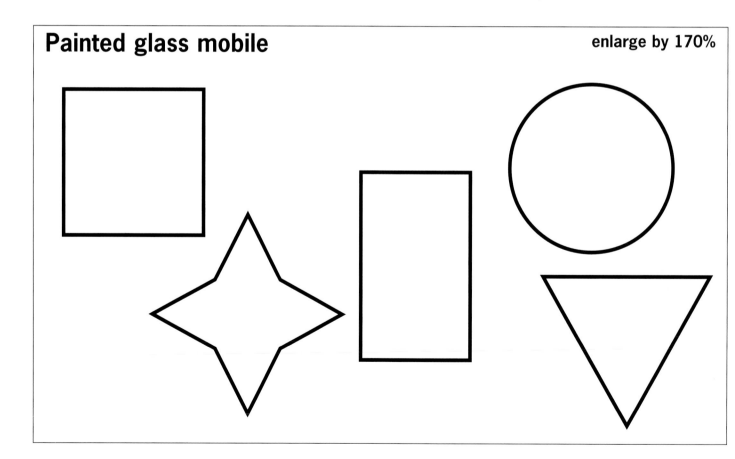

**Painted glass mobile**

enlarge by 170%

# Glossary

**Eyelets**

**Glass outliner**

**Jigsaw**

**Acetate sheets**
Used to cut stencils. Clear acetate sheets are placed on the design; trace directly onto the acetate using an acetate marker.

**Acorn**
A stop, normally made of wood or plastic, through which the strings of a blind are threaded and secured to keep them from coming undone.

**Acrylic paint**
Synthetic water-based paint. It is fast drying and can be diluted with water as required.

**Acrylic varnishing wax**
Water-based wax that can be applied with either a brush or a cloth. Once dry, it leaves a traditional waxy feel that can be buffed to a high gloss if required.

**All-purpose spackle**
Ideal for filling holes. Can be bought ready to use in a tube.

**Appliqué**
A fabric shape sewn on top of another fabric as decoration. It may be quilted.

**Batting**
A non-woven stuffing that can be cut into strips, rolled into tubes, or shredded to stuff awkward shapes.

**Chair rail**
A wooden rail—often of molding—at about waist height on an interior wall.

**Cleat**
Metal hook that is screwed to the window frame and around which you secure the cords from a blind.

**Color wash**
Very thin, almost transparent, layer of latex paint.

**Craft knife and cutting mat**
A professional knife used in conjunction with a special self-sealing cutting surface.

**Curtain weights**
Curtain weights are available as chains to lay along the hem or as button-shaped disks to secure in the corners.

**Dowel**
A narrow cylindrical rod of wood available in a range of diameters and lengths.

**Dust mask**
A mask that covers the nose and mouth to protect the wearer from inhaling dust.

**Eyelet hole punch**
Creates the right-sized hole in the fabric for a metal eyelet.

**Eyelets**
Metal rivets that you insert into a hole in fabric and hammer into place with a special tool.

**Gilding wax**
Ready-made metallic wax available in different finishes.

**Particle board**

**Sanding block**

**Stencil brush**

**Glass outliner**
Provides a contour line that hardens when dry.

**Glass paints**
Come in a variety of colors and can be diluted with lacquer thinner.

**Jigsaw**
A handheld electric saw that allows you to cut out shapes.

**Key**
To abrade a surface to provide it with a better grip on which paint can adhere when applied.

**Level**
A level used to figure out true vertical and horizontal directions.

**Nail-strength adhesive and caulking gun**
A high-strength adhesive that eliminates the need for nails and screws in many projects. It is applied with a standard caulking gun.

**Particle board**
A hard, dense material that has similar properties to solid wood. It comes in sheet form and has smooth surfaces on both sides, making it ideal to finish with paint.

**Piping**
Rounded edging that can be used on most soft furnishings.

**Piping cord**
Cord available in several widths; it is covered with fabric and helps to maintain the shape of the piping.

**Plastic-backed fabric**
Cotton that has been treated with a plastic coating on one side, providing a wipeable surface.

**Primer**
The first coat of paint, which protects the item and reduces absorption of further coats of paint.

**Sanding block**
Sandpaper wrapped around a wooden block.

**Spray adhesive**
An adhesive that does not give a permanent bond but allows lifting and repositioning.

**Spray polyurethane varnish**
A spray varnish that gives a tough plastic finish to surfaces, protecting them against scratches and abrasions. It resists staining from water and is available in satin or semigloss finishes.

**Stencil brush**
A stencil brush has short, stiff bristles and a chubby, wooden handle.

**Velcro**
The brand name for a hook and loop fastener. It consists of two pieces of nylon, one with tiny hooks and the other with small loops. The two sides adhere when pressed together.

**Wood glue**
A strong glue ideal for wood projects. A milky color, it dries to a clear finish.

# Suppliers

## GENERAL CRAFT

**Hobby Lobby**
7707 SW 44th Street
Oklahoma City, OK 73179
Tel: (405) 745-1100
www.hobbylobby.com

**Michaels Arts & Crafts**
8000 Bent Branch Drive
Irving, TX 75063
Tel: (214) 409-1300
www.michaels.com

**Zim's Crafts, Inc.**
4370 South 300 West
Salt Lake City, UT 84107
Toll free: (800) 453-6420
Tel: (801) 268-2505
Fax: (801) 268-9859
www.zimscrafts.com

## GENERAL ART SUPPLIES

**Jo-Ann Fabrics and Crafts**
www.joann.com
(website includes store locator)
Store questions: (888) 739-4120

## HARDWARE/ HOME IMPROVEMENT STORES

**Home Depot U.S.A., Inc.**
2455 Paces Ferry Road
Atlanta, GA 30339-4024
Tel: (770) 433-8211
www.homedepot.com

**Lowe's Home Improvement Warehouse**
Customer Care (ICS7)
Lowe's Companies, Inc.
P.O. Box 1111
North Wilkesboro, NC 28656
Toll free: (800) 44-LOWES
www.lowes.com

## PAINT PRODUCTS

**Delta Technical Coatings**
2550 Pellissier Place
Whittier, CA 90601
Toll free: (800) 423-4135
Fax: (562) 695-5157
www.deltacrafts.com
*Acrylic, glass, and fabric paints.*

**EK Success**
P.O. Box 1141
Clifton, NJ 07014-1141
Toll free: (800) 524-1349
success@eksuccess.com
www.eksuccess.com
*Paints and general craft products.*

**Pébéo of America**
P.O. Box 714
Route 78, Airport Rd.
Swanton, VT 05488
Toll free: (800) 363-5012
Fax: (819) 821-4151
*Glass paints, markers, and mediums.*

**Liquitex-Binney and Smith**
P.O. Box 431
Easton, PA 18044-0431
Tel: (888) 422-7954
www.liquitex.com
*Paints, mediums, varnishes, and additives.*

## PAINTBRUSHES

**Loew-Cornell**
563 Chestnut Ave.
Teaneck, NJ 07666-2490
Tel: (201) 836-7070
Fax: (201) 836-8110
www.loew-cornell.com

## FABRIC CRAFTS/NOTIONS

**Coats & Clark**
P.O. Box 27067
Greenville, NC 29616
Toll free: (800) 648-1479
www.coatsandclark.com
*General purpose threads.*

**Dharma Trading Co.**
P.O. Box 150916
San Rafael, CA 94915
Toll free: (800) 542-5227
catalog@dharmatrading.com
www.dharmatrading.com
*Fabric dyes, paints, and fabric art products.*

## STENCILS

**American Traditional Stencils**
442 First New Hampshire Turnpike
Northwood, NH 03261-3401
Tel: (603) 942-8100
www.americantraditional.com

**Royal Design Studio**
2504 Transportation Ave., Suite H
National City, CA 91950
Toll free: (800) 747-9767
www.royaldesignstudio.com

WI JUL 1 5 2002
4/13/04

# Index